OF THE
WOOD

OF THE
WOOD

Roy C Hammond

The Book Guild Ltd

First published in Great Britain in 2022 by
The Book Guild Ltd
Unit E2 Airfield Business Park,
Harrison Road, Market Harborough,
Leicestershire. LE16 7UL
Tel: 0116 2792299
www.bookguild.co.uk
Email: info@bookguild.co.uk
Twitter: @bookguild

Typeset in 11pt Adobe Jenson Pro

Printed on FSC accredited paper
Printed and bound in Great Britain by 4edge Limited

ISBN 978 1914471 643

British Library Cataloguing in Publication Data.
A catalogue record for this book is available from the British Library.

For Dad and Ollie

He was among trees then, spring trees tender with the new matchless green of young leaves, and a clear sun dappling them; summer trees full of leaf, whispering, massive; dark winter firs that fear no master and let no light brighten their woods. He learned the nature of all trees, the particular magics that are in oak and beech and ash.

The Dark Is Rising
Susan Cooper

Enter these enchanted woods,
You who dare.
Nothing harms beneath the leaves
More than waves a swimmer cleaves.
Toss your heart up with the lark.
Foot at peace with mouse and worm,
Fair you fare.
Only at dread of dark
Quaver, and they quit their form:
Thousand eyeballs under hoods
Have you by the hair.
Enter these enchanted woods,
You who dare.

The Woods of Westermain (excerpt)
George Meredith

CONTENTS

Part Three
Summer Wood

CONTENTS

Part Four
Autumn Wood

Part Five
Return to Winter Wood

PREFACE

I am a nemophilist; that is to say, I am a haunter of the woods, or rather one wood in particular, but occasionally others. 'My' wood is around 182 acres of perfect, mixed broadleaf and coniferous woodland enfolded by rolling Northamptonshire countryside. The wood is important to me; I grew up there and so too have my three children.

This record and the observations within are a thanks to the wood and everything it is and everything it has given me: stories, adventures, solitude, education, contemplation and reflection. It is all those things, and I cannot imagine life without it.

This is a journal of my observations of the wood's ebb and flow over a calendar year and a record of the story it has to tell over that year. We will see the wood change from its seemingly dormant winter state at the beginning of the year in the depth of the bleak winter, to the urgency of rapid spring growth and dazzling displays of myriad colour. We settle then into the long and dusty buzz of hot summer days, onto autumn bounty when the treetops weigh heavy and hedgerows are fit to burst, before a slow decline into a further period of rest.

I will not be able to visit the wood every day, but I will be there at least once a week.

Although I do hope you enjoy the read, this journal is selfishly, mainly for me. I have got my 'fix' of the wood most weeks for forty or so years, but there will inevitably come a time when I am no longer able to walk its paths and experience its wonders with my own eyes, but with this journal in hand, I can always be there.

Along with the odd story recent and old, and my observations and experiences of each visit, this journal will also be a voyage of discovery for me and perhaps you. Thanks to my dad, I know the names of the more common flora that call the wood home, those trees and plants that are the very essence of the fabric and character of the wood. But there are significant gaps in my knowledge, particularly of the delicate woodland floor plant species, some of which are indicators of just how old this lovely patch of English woodland is, perhaps standing for a thousand or so years. Armed with various field guides, I will do my best to give a name to the many plant species that I do not know.

I will also tell you something of our native animals, and less native animals, that rely on the wood for habitat, refuge and food, and at all times I will remember that I am a brief guest, an interloper in their world.

There is a little of the folklore associated with plants and trees – something of their uses and their magic that we have lost in our modern world. I think above all that is what draws me to the wood as often as I am allowed: that sense of timelessness.

More than anything, this is my experience of the wood

seen through amateur, but nevertheless enthusiastic and eager, eyes. Whilst I have tried to be accurate and authentic, there is a scattering of artistic license, and through a lack of knowledge, my descriptions, particularly of the woodland understorey plants and fungi, will be rather clumsy and there is inevitably misidentification.

Now a brief bit about my wood for context. It is a working wood; by that I mean that it is sensitively managed and harvested from time to time for its timber, including as part of good woodland management.

We can trace mention of a wood at Badby back to just before the Norman Conquest; Badby Wood was included in the assignment of villages of Badby and Newnham to Evesham Abbey by King Cnut in 1018 (he of the tide story). A couple of centuries later in 1246, King Henry III provided for the creation of a deer park at Badby Wood and granted the status of 'Free Warren' to the Abbot of Evesham, enabling the hunting and eating of the game of the wood. In 1542, Henry VIII passed the Fawsley Estate, including Badby Wood, to the Knightley Family of Fawsley. The estate remained in the family until the early part of the twentieth century.

The wood continues to be looked after and managed by the Fawsley Estate and they do a very good job of it.

If you have a wood near you, go out and find it; enter through its many doorways; stroll along its passageways; enjoy the vistas and surprises; and gaze up at its ceiling. Take in the sights, sounds and smells, and look in wonder at the animals that call it home.

If you become a frequent visitor, you will see its never-ending change from month to month, season to season and even hour by hour. Visit your wood at different times of day; it is a very different place at dawn from its atmosphere in the middle of the day and at its close. Be there in summer dry and winter storm. And especially in the gloaming – that is my favourite time, in the silvery light, enfolded by the cathedral of the wood, nestling somewhere between reality and dream. If magic exists anywhere in this land anymore, it is surely in the wood, in the falling light.

Before we begin our journey proper, please treat your wood with respect and as they say, take home only memories (and other people's litter) and leave only your footprints.

I hope you, the reader, enjoy this journal as much as I have enjoyed the journey.

Most importantly, leave the wood wild.

PART ONE
WINTER WOOD

ONE

OF THE ARCH
AND SQUIRRELS

Sunday, 6 January 2019 – 09.30

Here begins our journey.

There are many routes into the wood, and I have used them all to a lesser or greater extent over the years. Some now unfortunately have fallen into disuse through time or intention. This Sunday morning, I have chosen the most popular path into the wood, familiar to most visitors.

Until relatively recently, the small parking area where we leave the car stood in the deep shade of a clump of spreading mature horse chestnuts whose stretching boughs formed an entwined unbroken ceiling above. But they are long gone and now just a memory for us constant visitors.

The orange-hued track stretches out before us, tapering away in a sweeping curve to the dark band of wood ahead. We follow its path between barren fields and before very long we arrive at the ancient stone arch. My portal to the wild wood and its secrets.

The arch is as integral to the wood as its plants and beasts. It is the perfect ancient entrance to the wood. It is of red brick construction with ironstone ashlar facing. Ironstone is the natural local stone and predominant traditional building material hereabouts. The arch is Tudor in form and style with a battlement parapet. The head of the arch displays the coat of arms of the Knightley family, the carved detail now heavily eroded by the passing of years and the forces of ice and water. At one time, two squat stone gatehouses stood attached either side, providing a grand entrance to the estate and deer park; they are sadly long gone and no visible trace remains, save for the occasional shard of blue and white pottery flecking the muddy surface of the path. Nature has reclaimed hungrily memories and all the space their stonework once occupied.

Upon entering the wood, the first of the disturbed grey squirrels we will encounter today agilely claws its way up the nearest oak to our right, moving out of view from our unwelcome intrusion. The grey squirrel – cousin to our native red – does not hibernate during the winter months, instead remaining active, dipping into its cache of acorns and chestnuts dotted around and about, carefully hidden away in the rich loam throughout the busy late summer and quieter autumn months.

It must be at this time of year that the boar, as the males are known, will seek out a sow for the spring litter. I know that they are much maligned, and I dare say I would rather see a native red, but I quite like their agile antics, and they are constant companions, always keeping their distance from human interlopers.

As I have said, I will share some of my stories of the wood with you from time to time and right now, I am reminded of a brush with a squirrel in the wood some years ago.

Back when Ollie and I were much younger and fitter, we would go for a run up the wood most summer evenings. This one particular evening, I had a very close call with a less than agile grey. Lost in thought, and with Ollie panting in full four-legged stride along the woodland path beside me (unusually actually – most of the time he would be somewhere out of sight, moving less than quietly through the undergrowth on the trail of something or other) he, that being the squirrel, fell a matter of inches from my nose to land, limbs splayed flat, on the summer dry path in front of me.

For a very short while, we three – a dog, a human and unwitting squirrel – shared a moment of jarring surprise. Myself struggling to process what I was seeing, Ollie apparently largely the same, and the free fall squirrel presumably stunned and a little winded. But our shared stupor lasted only fractions of a second more, before the squirrel, none the worse for wear, but maybe with pride dented, was up on his tiny, clawed feet and off at blurring speed in amongst the trunks and the tangles of the bramble to our right. The squirrel was closely followed by an excited and very vocal Ollie in pursuit, having regained his wits, with absolutely no hope of bagging it. Seconds more later, the squirrel had found safe refuge somewhere out of sight, and an impotent Ollie looked as confused and as harmless as ever. I should not think a squirrel landing at your feet from height is an everyday occurrence.

Before us is the main path dividing the wood that must have been a well-used route from Fawsley Hall and its parkland through the wood and on to the village beyond. The partly metalled surface of glimpsed broken masonry hints at its use as a regular thoroughfare for gentlemen and ladies on horseback, or perhaps even in smart horse-drawn carriage or coach.

The main track is flanked by coppiced hazel hereabouts, left unruly now, and dotted at regular intervals. Each late summer, the clusters of green unripened hazelnuts are taken early by too eager squirrels, and we have yet to try a sufficiently ripened nut from the wood. The hazel tree is identifiable in the winter by its smooth grey-brown bark and catkins. Coppiced hazel stems make excellent and robust walking sticks, as well as hurdles, withy fencing and wattle.

We know from archaeological investigations that roasted hazelnuts were a staple diet of our ancient hunter gatherer ancestors, perhaps foraged and eaten by our pre-history forefathers in search of wisdom. The male flowers, known as catkins, appear in distending clusters along the bare, spreading branches in the autumn but do not open out fully to ensure future generations until the warmer spring.

As we make our way along the ancient track, as is often the case at this time of year, we are chastised by a large flock of foraging great tits flitting about and between the interconnecting network of leafless branches of hazel and beech overhead. The great tits' size and distinctive black crown, black neck and throat and striking white cheeks make it one of our easier native birds to identify. Leaving their alarm calls behind, and with no sign of the rain they foretell, we push deeper into the welcome embrace of the wood and its secrets and surprises.

I enjoy all times of year and seasons up the wood, but it is fair to say that you do not see the wood in all its glory in the midwinter. It is a resting time, in anticipation of the spring to come beyond the horizon and of productive months. The deciduous trees – the oaks, sweet chestnut and beech – are stripped bare; the woodland floor is a carpet of fallen leaves of all shapes and sizes, which have lost their rich autumn hues, giving way to a carpet of dirty lighter and darker browns. The understorey plants and their mosaic of spring and summer colour have long since died down. The only splash of colour providing scant relief are the deep greens provided by the odd patch of late bracken. Although typically a moor or heath species, bracken, alongside bramble, is the prevalent ground cover species in the wood and, if left unchecked, can begin to choke the ground to shoulder height at full growth, to the detriment of other understorey species. If you are interested, the origin of the word 'bracken' is old Scandinavian from the Swedish *braken* and Danish *bregne*, both of which mean *fern*.

In a survival situation, not that you are ever likely to be so in lowland English woodland, the young bracken fronds, known as 'fiddleheads', are a source of food. Though, the British Royal Horticultural Society recommends against consumption.

After a while, and keeping to the main path, ignoring the multitude of the other lesser paths diverging away and tapering between trunks, we arrive at what is probably my most favourite spot, at which I, and whoever is with me, never fail to stop for a few moments of quiet contemplation. It is a five-bar field gate of smooth, worn timber, located at the southern end of the main track where woodland transitions abruptly into the open landscaped parkland of the estate. The view from here is of aged parkland and ancient sentinel oaks dotted throughout the grassland and broad patches of winter brown bracken. This view is of managed English landscape at its very best. As good as any landscape and vista in the world. Partially hidden, we have glimpses here between the leafless oaks and their robust trunks and spreading rambling crowns of the ruin of the Dower House away in the distance. We will take some time later to learn a bit more about its history.

Beyond the park to the south, rolling Northamptonshire countryside and its network of ordered hedgerows enclosing fields of pasture and ploughed orangey soil stretches out to the distant horizon; bolder greens in the foreground give way to terraced ever lighter misty greys.

With thoughts of predatory hawking dragonflies, a long way from emerging, and foraging bats on black wing, now hibernating for the winter, we reluctantly leave the parkland vista behind and turn left to follow the now southern edge of the wood.

Passing through the firs, we are back into semi-mature and mature beech; the younger trees, waiting patiently below their naked parents, are dressed still in golden leaves. The air today is still, but on a breezy winter's day, the dry beech leaves rattle and rustle noisily in the icy air, broadcasting a white noise backdrop to the secret language of the wood.

The path here steadily rises in a westerly direction, following the natural topography. After ten or so minutes, and at a gentle pace, we emerge from the beech trees to what must be an ancient route or trackway into the wood from the parkland beyond. Situated between steep banks, a hollow way descends steeply into the wood. We often stopped at this spot with Dad, taking a minute to rest and to admire the Great Beech – a once important landmark in my wood – its height and canopy spread accentuated by its lofty position at the top of the deer bank. Sadly, four or so years ago, on our return from an overseas adventure, we discovered our Great Beech toppled across the hollow way, strength and majesty having succumbed to age, decay and the forces of nature. What a sight and sound it must have been to have witnessed its fall.

All is silent and still now, and already a fern has made its home in the hollow ragged stump. The once open hollow way has become choked with bramble and bracken competing for space below the mighty prone trunk dotted with mouldering fungi, altering this micro-landscape. As good an example as any of the wood as a living and ever-changing entity. The sister to the Great Beech, however, still stands nearby, its one side largely bare, testament to the dominance of its once larger sister.

Life in the wood goes on. Not far from the ragged stump, a wiry beech sapling, no more than shin height, grows strong and healthy, and in three hundred or so years, if time and the fates allow, it may match the majesty of its parent.

The Great Beech was also one of Dad's favourite spots. Something of him rests here now.

Now, normally we would descend all the way into the valley to the north and head into the heart of the wood, centred around Hazley Knobb (or Knobbly Knott as Dad used to call it). But not today. Instead, we continue along the southern edge of the wood, through the lighter and darker browns, with the steep-sided deer bank rising to our left. Accompanied by the laugh of the woodpecker, we gradually descend into one of the wetter areas of the wood, where narrow clear running streams converge in deep-sided banks, threading their way through thickets of hazel. If not careful, the less aware are apt to lose a shoe or worse still, their footing hereabouts. Clay must be the main shallow geology here, below the humus, and the cracking of the ground, evidence of last year's very dry and hot summer, is still clearly visible.

From the streams we ascend the northern edge of the wood, with glimpses of rolling pasture to our left, out beyond the wood edge, and past the ash whips and through clumps of self-set holly, noticeable in this part of the wood. Blowing a little at the steady ascent along the gently meandering path, we arrive back at the ancient stone arch and our exit back to the modern world.

TWO

OF THE WIND
AND THE DARK

Sunday, 13 January 2019 – 07.05

An early wood walk this morning. The wood does not generally get busy at this time of year, but it is still nice to get there early, with the knowledge that for a short while at least the wood and its expanse and solitude is yours.

We park up in the early morning winter dark and take the main route in, passing through the timber kissing gates, which clack carelessly behind. The wind is blowing hard this early Sunday morning – not quite a gale but not far off – clutching at coats and buffeting exposed skin and hair. The yellowing grass either side of the narrow track nods in waves and ripples, bowing to the wind. There is just a hint of tentative first light on the easterly horizon glimpsed below the heavy grey cloud – a line of thin orange fire, Mordor-like.

Soon after passing to the side of the arch and with some trepidation, we are enfolded by the dark of the interior. The dark and strong persistent wind gives the wood a brooding and wild character this morning. We turn immediately left off the main path and follow the long northern edge. The wind rushes through the barely silhouetted canopies overhead and causes trunks to sway and bare branches to clatter (I have worried about what I will write in each entry, sufficient to hold your interest, but it turns out I have just to let the wood speak to me).

There are no beasts to be seen or heard yet this morning within the confines of the wood; they take wise shelter in deep earthen burrows and dense thorny thickets out of sight.

We continue along the hardpacked path and into the conifers, where the dark and shadow holds sway over the probing light.

As a young boy up the wood with my dad, the pines and firs were my favourite part of the wood, promising fantasy adventure and enchantment. Even in the middle of the brightest day, below the dense fragrant evergreen canopies, it was always gloomy, the woodland floor deep in shade and shadow. It is easy for young boys amongst the gloom to imagine mythical beasts and child-catching monsters just out of sight, keeping pace, flitting between trunks and cowering behind fallen giants on the hunt. Fear not! There was always a fallen branch to be had on the woodland floor just perfect for sword or spear, ready for courageous attack and defence.

The mature dark green needle-shaped leaves of the firs have a strong and clean pine smell when rubbed vigorously between hands. I have read that the needles make good tea, but I have never tried it.

I have camped a couple of times in the wood as a young teenager hereabouts, in amongst the cover of the firs. I am quite sure we were not supposed to, and it is not something that I would encourage now. The world has moved on since the early 1980s and the wood is privately owned.

Accompanied by complaining blackbirds, we continue through the half-light up and into the high beeches and into the eastern side of the wood. At this spot we are elevated, with the wooded ground falling away steadily either side. The wind blows hard through the mast-straight grey trunks.

All around is the alarming sound of the roaring wind clattering branch against branch.

We linger only briefly at the five-bar gate overlooking the parkland and continue on, dropping down the well-trodden path into further firs. From here and to our left there is a good, although distant, view out from the wood edge across the parkland – still in the half-light – to the brick stacks, stone gables and polygonal tower of the ancient ruin. As with the wood and the arch, I have known the Dower House for most of my life. It holds as much interest for me today as it did at eight years old when unburdened imagination ran wild. What stories would it tell if it were able?

Continuing on in the tempest, a large flock of erratic jackdaws passes swiftly overhead, riding the very edge of the living wind and adding to the silhouettes of the canopies against the lightening sky. Did you know, because I did not, that a flock of jackdaws is called a *train*? Appropriate for the locomotive rush of the wind this morning.

Apart from the ever-prevailing wind, the remainder of our walk through the trees is uneventful. We emerge into full light around eight-thirty, dishevelled and with tea and bacon butties in mind.

THREE

OF SOUND
AND SILENCE

Sunday, 20 January 2019 – 15.35

My youngest daughter and I set out to the wood today with the objective of keeping quiet, moving stealthily along the woodland paths, hoping to steal glimpses of some of the larger fleet-footed beasts. Normally, early morning, or last light, is a good time to see some of the larger mammals, such as the roe deer which once inhabited the wood in great numbers. The reality is you never quite know what you will experience and often the wood has seemingly pre-planned surprises. Every trip to the wood is an adventure!

We arrive, we two, a little under an hour from an early winter sunset. The air is a frigid four degrees under a grey sky and there is not a breath of wind to stir bare, dark branches.

We park up in the normal spot along with more cars than I thought there would be at this time of the day (and perhaps more than I would like) and make our way along the main track, past the arch and off along the northern edge, heading east.

Today is about the quiet and stillness. A wood holding its breath, in winter rest. Sometimes the wood is like that, and at such times, you feel compelled to whisper and tread the paths lightly in reverence. The damp ground and multitude trunks keep sound close and confined. When the wood is dormant and still, that is the best time for contemplation, for the clearing of a cluttered, busy mind, while the wood and its children look on. This is my church and I wonder if the old gods are listening?

The only interruption to the silence is the delicate whistle of the ever-present tits and the jarring, repetitive 'bicycle pump' call of the great tit nearby. Alongside the 'pink pink pink pink' alarm call of a pair of blackbirds who, despite our stealth, were clearly more aware of our presence far sooner than we were of theirs. I give the impression of a backdrop of birdsong and call, but in the main, all is still.

We move quietly up through the firs and into the high beeches before dropping down to the now familiar gateway, where as normal, we while away a few minutes. Just listening and chatting about matters important to vital teenage daughters but less important to their long-suffering fathers. The comfortable quiet is disturbed by the jackdaws, calling to each other in the parkland oaks to gather the *train* together for the roost before dark.

I have over the last couple of years thought, very occasionally, that I had heard the deep throaty croak of a raven up the wood but with a good deal of scepticism; they are, after all, a bird more at home in the wild high places of the north and west. But after today, I am more convinced because, not only did we hear that same resonate croak for the first time since last summer, but this time we were also able to see him or her; a solitary dark bird, jet black plumage, flies towards us, between the sentinel oaks and into the wood edge to our right. Noticeably larger than the crow, and with a distinctive whoosh of each glossy wing beat, he soars past. I think I will name him 'Bran, the Keeper of the Wood'.

With the light fading, and a return to stillness and silence, we turn left, back into the dense firs and shortly after, onto the snaking, steadily rising path winding its way through the young and old beech. Turning right at the splintered ruin of the Great Beech, we drop by the side of the hollow way into the heart of the wood and to the toe of Knobbly Knott. Its southern wooded slope ascends before us.

After a short climb, we make our way through the now died down understorey to the summit. Knobbly Knott is another landmark of the wood. Not quite the centre, but you have the strong sense that it is. A number of the wood's paths converge upon it and radiate out again in equal fashion. The Knott holds a lofty position and provides a circular break in the otherwise continuous canopy.

I have watched the top change over the years; once fully open and grassed, the bracken, bramble and wild raspberry are stealthily taking over, creeping imperceptibly so that pathways are narrowed and choked, clawing at passers-by. Only a small, open, grassed area remains now, in amongst the mature beech and solitary oak and juvenile sweet chestnut. A couple of stumps of long-forgotten monoliths provide handy resting places. The ants, solitary bees and crickets are long gone, awaiting the return of the warmer months.

Knobbly Knott, with its flat top and long sweeping slopes, has always been a place of play and gathering. You are never too old for a rope swing. Decades old, long-forgotten frayed ropes hang forlornly high out of reach, entirely still, in the absence of even the slightest breeze. But, as there nearly always is, one swing remains within reach, carrying on the long tradition and full of youthful promise.

There is a level area, a short way down the northern slope, now occupied by a sett and maturing hollies. A long time ago, before the responsibilities of adulthood and the distractions of modern life, myself and friends camped here a couple of times. Armed with canvas tents, Primus stoves and plentiful tins of beans, we did things that all children should do: out in the wild, away from technology and still with an irrational fear of the dark. We shared stories of white ladies and headless horsemen, along with laughter and the making of memories.

Jim Bob and I rest awhile, settling on the exposed gnarled root of the largest beech at the top. All around us underfoot are littered fallen beech nut husks, generally without fruit. We wait for a glimpse of the family of badgers that we often see in the falling light. Badgers often have secondary setts that they occupy at different times of the year, or in times of danger, and I wonder if they are now abroad elsewhere. Another time, when we are able to observe their nervous first steps for their night-time ramblings, at respectful distance, we will learn more about them.

We are losing the light fast now, and we have another twenty minutes or so before we will be back where we began. We descend the long, and in places steep, northern slope deeper into the heart of the wood. Past the confluence of streams and on to the northern edge. With the lilting, soulful song of a hidden robin bidding us farewell, we make our way out past the arch and into the twilight. The distant bells of Badby church chime five o'clock.

Of note today, I did notice that the honeysuckle, entwined around an unsuspecting trunk, is starting to leaf up a little, tentative early new growth. I may have also spotted the first delicate green shoots of a bluebell emerging out of the loam and leaf litter. They are a promise of spring and new life, still a little way off.

I yearn to bring you stories and descriptions of the wood in deep winter, of low-lying mists, of frosts and hard, frozen ground, and if Mother Nature has good grace, of a wood deep in blanketing snow. But that is all for another time. Hopefully.

FOUR

OF THE FOX

Monday, 28 January 2019 – late afternoon

The late afternoon is cold, and a slight breeze stirs the yellowed grasses. The muddy, gravelled path of the main track stretches out before me, leading up to the dark mass of the wood. The surface of the path has that arid appearance that you sometimes see at this time of year, where the frigid dry air has drawn the very last of the moisture from the cold, hard ground.

The sky is a steely flat grey, and the fields either side are barren. The cultivated earth either side of the track is hard to the touch, without a dusting of frost. The landscape is all winter browns and blacks and greys. As I draw near to the arch, I can see the skeletal trees either side. A pair of crows drift lazily above the bare canopies, black against the grey.

The interior of the wood is still, listless and melancholy. I make my way steadily along the main track, without haste, to the five-bar gate and rest awhile. I skirt the southern edge, heading west, up through the beeches, still orange leafed. What light there is, is retreating.

Far away, through the acres of the wood, some beast screeches to the end of the day, jarring my distant musings. The remote sound has a haunting, lonely quality. Ageless instinct raises fine hairs on my arms and back of my neck. Our forefathers, with only the benefit of a fearful imagination and absence of scientific explanation, might well have closed shutters and barred planked doors against such a ghoulish noise on the very edge of the dark.

But this is today, and whilst the bark of the fox is not a pleasant sound (especially close to sundown), it is a perfectly natural and familiar noise of the British countryside. Foxes bark, or rather screech, more at this time of year in search of a mate and to call out territories.

It is cold and nearly full dark when I make my way back to the car, perhaps with a little more haste than is necessary.

FIVE

OF SNOW AND ICE

Saturday, 2 February 2019 – 07.30

The following is mostly a transcript of a voice recording I made of my trip to the wood early Saturday, 2 February.

A different route into the wood this morning.

I park up in Church Green, within the confines of the village. One of the many greens in Badby village and overlooked by the Church of St Mary the Virgin. The Knightley Way begins at this point, taking the walker down a narrow, descending path between squat Northamptonshire stone cottages. I make my way between the cottages and down the relatively steep valleyside, heading south. I am accompanied by a rooster crowing nearby to the first light. Two blackbirds fly ahead and there is the clatter of pigeon wings in the bare canopies to my right, their slumber disturbed by my passage.

The ground underfoot is frozen hard and in places, dusted by a light covering of snow.

A solitary ewe is hunkered down to my left, tucked in against the tired fleece-strewn stock fence and in amongst the cover of the hedgerow. The ewe is unconcerned by my passing but keeps a wary lookout from its lofty position all the same.

The path I am following is noticeably sunken between the pasture either side and the hedgerows crowd in, coming together above me, creating a natural tunnel. I reach the valley bottom and pass over one of the headwaters of the river Nene – a small, barely flowing trickle of a stream at this point. I reach the first timber kissing gate on the opposite side of the valley. An old, battered Knightley Way sign leans forlorn at an angle in the hedgerow, soon to be lost to Spring growth. Beyond the kissing gate, the path opens out into close grazed pasture. The edge of our wood lies a hundred yards or so ahead.

It is very cold this morning and the ground is hard and crisp underfoot. The weatherman delivered on his promise, and we did have snow, the last remnants of which lie in small patches in hollow and shade. I turn right and after a short while reach a second kissing gate; this normally muddy spot is frozen hard. Beyond the gate, a clear path of hardpacked snow stretches out in front of me. My boots crump and I follow in the footsteps of rabbits, dogs and other walkers. The ever-present tits call to each other from within the wood nearby. It is not quite the knee-deep polar trek that I had hoped for, but it is still very definitely a winter's morning.

So, I follow the white path leading us on into the distance through tufts of frost-touched grasses and ice-capped molehills. I pass through the final kissing gate and into the north-western corner of the wood.

The only snow to be seen within the wood lies along the lengths of fallen trunks dotted about. Ignoring the Knightley Way heading south, I take the path to the left through the dry ditch and in the direction of the streams. The woodland floor is hard underfoot and the frozen leaf litter and less-than-careful footfalls make stealth impossible. I pass over a running stream and to my left is one of the other entrances into the wood via a wooden footbridge; I must have been past it a thousand times but have never used it; we will soon. Something large and heavy is disturbed ahead, making its way quickly deeper into the wood, unseen and in anxious flight.

I descend down and over the converging streams, without incident. On the opposite bank, I take a second to stand still to listen to the jackdaws and tom tits, before turning right and following a further dry stream bed. It really is very difficult to be quiet this morning; my passage is a constant crackle and crunch over the frozen leaf-strewn ground.

After a short time, I arrive at the painter's crossroads (more about him another time). A path stretches off in either direction to the left and right, traversing the wood east and west, highlighted this morning in white. There is birdsong all around while I keep straight ahead and start to ascend the long, northern slope of Knobbly Knott. I may have just heard the delicate bell-like song of a wren somewhere amongst the understorey. The cold is starting to bite at the end of exposed extremities. About halfway up the northern slope of the Knott, the tree cover opens up a little, allowing for longer views, and the top of the Knott can be seen in the distance.

The top, when I arrive, is breezy and cold and snow-covered. The cold breeze stirs the brown leaves on the lower branches of the mature oak crowning the summit. Every twig of the oak has new buds, pent up energy waiting for the return of the longer days not too far off.

I keep going through the snow, crumping underfoot. In the centre of the summit clearing, the wood surrounds you in a 360-degree panorama. It is a timeless winter scene.

A woodpecker hammers at a tree nearby, and a buzzard mews somewhere in the distance. It is only now, in writing this journal, that I take the time to stop and observe and properly listen to the life and beating heart of the wood that surrounds and enfolds me in a welcome and familiar embrace.

I drop down the southern slope, still serenaded by the hammering of the woodpecker. The dark edge of the stand of firs is away to my left, and ahead, the deer bank defining the southern edge to this part of the wood is blanketed in snow this morning.

I start to rise in the direction of the Great Beech, passing small scrapes on the woodland floor, evidence of foraging squirrels, and turn right at the base of the hollow way, heading west along the southern edge. At some point, I must take you along the top of the deer bank, although there is no defined path. Dad and I walked along the top once and disturbed a resting adder or grass snake, basking in the sun. All a very long time ago.

After a short while I enter a glade where the trunks and canopies are less dense and where grasses and bracken make the most of the opportunity to establish themselves in large swathes. This spot has always been a frost pocket, more exposed to the cold without the benefit of tree cover. Consequently, there is more snow in this glade this morning compared to the remainder of the wood. The glade is quite beautiful; oranges and browns contrast sharply with the bright winter white.

I continue on, following in the footsteps of dogs and fellow walkers along the snowy path. Off to my left, at the top of the deer bank, the trunks of the sycamores and wild cherry are silhouetted black, but the early sun paints the canopy tops in golden first light. A solitary silver birch stands in solitude amongst the sycamores to my right, its silvery white bark providing relief to the surrounding darker tones. Here, it is quiet with little birdsong, just the rush of the chill breeze in my ears.

To my left, and located about halfway along the western half of the southern edge, is the second sett of the wood, and I make my way up the bank off the path for a closer look. The snow cover makes it easy to see the clear five-toed badger prints and criss-cross pattern of travel from opening to opening and radiating out into the wider wood, along well-established game trails. I worry that they know I am here, so I move on and leave them to their rest. I wonder if this is the same family which occupies the sett on Knobbly Knott?

I pass the point at which the Knightley Way leaves the wood and heads out into the parkland and continue on along the southern edge. The rising bank is to my left and the deep ditch is to my right. I wonder if these natural features have been modified and accentuated to discourage the deer from leaving the wood?

A bit about an oddity of the wood now, positioned next to the path adjacent to the western edge. It is not something that has been in the wood for a very long time, but it is now well established and a familiar, curious feature. It is hard to describe and probably means different things to different people and may mean something very specific to someone or some family.

For me, it has the feel of a shrine, and I will tell you now something of the eclectic collection of offerings that it comprises; there is a little table, or stool, at the base of what is a large sweet chestnut. The stool nestles in a natural hollow enfolded by the buttress roots of the chestnut towering behind and above. On top of the table, or altar, are arranged a haphazard mismatched collection of toys and other offerings – there is Lego, a plastic toy moose (the only moose you are ever likely to see up the wood), a metal racing car, key ring, pen, reel of bright red cotton, lorry, motorbike, pirate in a glass jar, a Minion and two small tins; both tins are filled to the brim with coppers and the odd silver coin. And dotted about the fallen branches, purposefully fashioned into an arch over the altar, are tied coloured ribbons, teddy bears and a wind chime with the face of a Green Man (appropriate for the wood). It is all very odd and intriguing.

When you pass the shrine – if that's what it is – you feel compelled to carry on the tradition of making an offering, in the same way that when you are in the fells and pass a waymarking cairn, you feel compelled to add to the jumbled pile of guiding rocks. But, this morning, armed with just my car key, I make the humble offering of a fallen brown sweet chestnut leaf, placing it with reverence at the base of the stool. My own offering to whatever or whoever. The shrine is entirely out of place and jarring, but I like it all the same and remain fascinated. It fits somehow, as odd as it is.

I leave the shrine to the gods of the wood behind and continue on over the frozen ground. Despite several layers, I am starting to feel the chill now and so pick up the pace a little. I drop down now to our exit, along the Knightley Way, clearly picked out in a white band flanked by the darker fallen leaves either side.

Birdsong has returned and is all around, including a great tit, singing from its broad repertoire of calls. I can just see to my left my favourite of all the birds, darting lightly in amongst the tangle of the hedgerow branches. So small, it can only be the very tiny wren, short tail held high. Not just one but a pair and complaining quietly about being disturbed.

I am at the western edge now, where views are possible out over the pasture. The Plantation and Down away to the west are picked out in early sunshine on the near horizon. Rolling snow-dusted hills are visible in the distance.

A buzzard calls again, still out of sight. We will hear and see more of the buzzards soon, as they catch the rising warm air over the Summer Wood, ascending in graceful spirals.

I continue to drop down the western edge, along a metalled path of deliberate brick and stone. Badby church is just visible in front of me, with its stumpy rectangular tower. I arrive at the kissing gate at the north-western corner. One of the posts is curiously inlaid with four coins, their edges hammered deep into the ringed grain.

On exiting, a cautious and ownerless wire-haired fox terrier bids me farewell.

SIX

OF THE DAWN

Sunday, 3 February 2019 – 06.50

The second visit to the wood of the weekend. It is Sunday morning. Cold and dark. I am joined by the old friend this early morning. We take the same route in as my lone walk yesterday. Yesterday's entry was about observation and experience; this morning, the time is filled with idle conversation and comfortable silence.

Once in the wood, we follow generally the same route as yesterday but with a very slight detour in the direction of Knobbly Knott. We stop briefly to admire the perfectly formed myriad squirrel tracks along the top of a fallen snow-covered trunk. Nature's highway. In no time, we are at the summit, still snow-capped and frigid. The sky is lightening all the time.

I can bring you news of the owl for the first time now; we can hear the call of the tawny owl, some distance away but no less magnificent. We shall hear it again, and I shall tell you more then. We may even speak a little with the owls if we are lucky.

We drop down the southern slope, over the obstacle course of snow and ice-covered fallen trunks. Instead of heading to the Great Beech, we turn left and skirt the northern edge of the stand of firs, their gloomy interior lost in shadow. A robin, with its distinctive redbreast, scouts ahead, alighting and flying in short hops along the path in front of us. We are following a path I regularly walked when my children were much younger, but it has fallen out of use now and will soon be entirely lost to the ever-encroaching bramble.

After a while, with the bramble in ascendency, we double back and follow the southern edge of the wood heading west, where we spot a fox; just a brief glimpse of rusty red coat heading up and over the deer bank and into the parkland. He is quickly lost to sight.

A short while later and the wood edge opens up a little to our left as the deer bank gradually peters out. The first light of the just risen sun washes the trunks ahead in golden winter orange. We take a little time to stop and gaze out from the confines of the wood across the parkland – the ruin stands lonely and silent in the distance surrounded by white and brown frosted grassland. We have heard the call of the green woodpecker a couple of times this morning, along with its machine-gun pecking, but now, we also get to see him; he darts from the cover of the wood to our left and alights on the twisted limb of a gnarly parkland oak a hundred or so yards in front of our position. He knows we are here and retreats quickly to the opposite side of the trunk out of view; I find them to be a secretive and shy bird.

We carry on and after leaving the wood, we follow the intimate sunken path back up to the church and its squat finialed tower. A reclusive song thrush lost to the trunks and the tangles keeps us company for a time with its rolling farewell song.

> *At once a voice arose among*
> *The bleak twigs overhead*
> *In a full-hearted evensong*
> *Of joy illimited;*
> *An aged thrush, frail, gaunt, and small,*
> *In blast-beruffled plume,*
> *Had chosen thus to fling his soul*
> *Upon the growing gloom.*

The Darkling Thrush (excerpt)
Thomas Hardy

Not quite befitting of the early hour but beautiful all the same.

SEVEN

OF THE RAIN

Sunday, 10 February 2019 – 10.05

It rained hard overnight, filling gutters and glistening sodium-lit pavements.

I laid awake and restless in the early hours in our loft room listening to its steady staccato beat overhead on old grey slates. It had not let up by morning and I have to confess as to struggling for motivation, but by mid-morning, the call of the wood and the need to continue its story was just too strong.

On my own, I arrive in the persistent rain mixed with biting driven sleet. The track up to the arch is more stream than path in places. Miniature orange rivulets rush between, around and over miniature pebbled rapids. My worn boots splash and scatter airborne droplets glistening ahead.

Once in the wood, I turn right instead of the by now familiar left. It is time to mix it up a bit, I think, and see familiar landmarks of the wood from new perspectives.

Today, it is about the rain; it is a steady hiss and patter all around. White droplets bejewel pensive buds, and twisted branches and trunks are stained a darker shade facing into the weather. Other trunks glisten, adding shine to the smooth bark. I head west into the prevailing weather, hands tucked deep into pockets and protective hood pulled down low.

The birds and the beasts are largely quiet this rainy morning, driven to cover and shelter by the weather, but there is just the odd call of the energetic tit nearby and the echoey hammering of an industrious woodpecker somewhere in the distance.

I drop down to the streams, swollen by the rain, their waters heavy with coloured sediment.

Near to the western edge, I turn south and take a path running parallel to the southern edge but set a couple of hundred yards in and at a lower level. I catch a fleeting glimpse of a buzzard flying low on silent riffling wings through the bare canopies; it is lost to view almost as soon as spotted (I wonder what else I miss, if not looking in the right direction and at the right time). The buzzard's generally brown and sandy, almost unruly plumage, together with its size, make it easy to identify. The sighting of a buzzard up the wood and its distinctive mewing call is now commonplace; I am sure the red kites are not far behind.

The sound of Badby church bells tolling in the village are carried to me pleasantly through the trees and the rain.

After a while, I come across a further oddity of the wood; it is a large stand of ancient rhododendron sprawling its tangled mass of dark brown limbs and waxy evergreen leaves for a hundred yards or so over the woodland floor and well below the canopies of the surrounding sycamore and oak. Entirely alien, it must have been planted intentionally; rhododendron is, after all, not native to English woodland or indeed the British Isles. I wonder who planted it and when? We will visit the rhododendron again in the spring where we may see it in full bloom. It is an interloper and out of place, particularly in these fallow months, but it is still beautiful in flower.

I continue along the path, very wet but generally firm underfoot, and after a short while the western slope of Knobbly Knott emerges by degrees into view; its western flank is painted shades of gold by last autumn's fallen leaves. The path I am following skirts in a long, sweeping arc around its south-western quarter.

I startle a resting muntjac deer from its well-defended shelter out of the rain under a lone holly; I spy only the dazzling bright white of its rump bounding away into the dense cover of bracken and bramble ahead. The muntjac is also not native but is now common and frequently seen in the Midlands' countryside. It is a noticeably small species of deer hailing originally from Asia and has curious tusks, long, sloping, marked face, terminating in a disproportionately large nose below stumpy antlers.

I turn right away from the alure of the Knott and in the direction of the Great Beech but do not quite get that far, deciding on a whim instead to take a more minor shortcut off to the left, where after a short while, I join the main path following the southern edge. I continue on in the acres of wood in the persistent and pattering rain.

I pass the five-bar gateway to the parkland and head up to the south-eastern corner. It is a more remote part of the wood out of the way and off the more popular paths. It is as a result less well visited, and I myself am an infrequent visitor to this part of the wood. I come across an ancient sett here, excavated into the natural slope. Years, maybe even decades and centuries, of excavated orange soil and ironstone rubble form substantial spoil terraces stepped down the long slope. There are obvious signs of recent activity and I make a mental note to make a return dusk visit.

My last encounter this morning is with Bran, flying on black glossy wings just above the canopy and towards me from the west. He croaks a farewell as I leave the wood. The rain has eased considerably to only a few spots carried in the westerly winds as I emerge.

By the time I am back home, bright blue sky can be glimpsed and there is welcome winter sunshine between ragged cloud.

Of note this morning, and a change from last weekend, countless thousands of bluebell shoots begin to carpet every centimetre of the woodland floor, with a promise of new life and vigour and an end to the darker months.

EIGHT

OF NEW DISCOVERIES

Sunday, 17 February 2019 – 07.10

A new route into the wood this morning; one I have never used before. The old friend keeps me company.

We park up at the greens in the village and walk down Chapel Lane under a cloudless blue sky. There is a footpath on the right, just after the robust red-brick chapel and the entrance to Brookside Lane. We pass through a kissing gate where the path leads up and over the growing pasture where it runs parallel to Brookside Lane for a time. The path is well walked and not just by us humans; there are cloven muntjac deer tracks to be seen imprinted into the damp orangey brown Northamptonshire soil.

Once past the neatly arranged and tended graves to our right, and after a bit of a climb, our wood comes into view. At this point there are impressive, elevated views out over the tops of the bare skeletal canopies, before the sweep of wood follows the landform rising up to the far wooded horizon.

I have not seen the wood from this spot before and it is the highlight of today's visit. It will become a familiar passageway into the magic of the wood.

NINE

OF THE WILD

The view from the car on the way to the wood is of the Nene valley laid out below us, shrouded in fog under a blue sky. Just the tops of the tallest oak and ash poke hazily through the grey-white covering. The dark band of the wood dominates the horizon in the far distance.

The bare blackthorn is just starting to flower in the hedgerows either side of the narrow country lane; the small white flowers contrast sharply with the dark brown, almost black bark of the thorny branches and trunks. The blackthorn in the autumn will gift us with a harvest of sloes for Christmas 2020. The hard thumbnail-sized fruits are purple in colour, with a dusty velvety covering and have a strong astringent taste apt to suck the very last of the moisture from tongue and gums – the fruit is best left for the gin.

Another new route this morning and another one I have not used for nearly forty years. We follow a ridge of high ground, the land falling away gradually each side, along a clear, well-worn orangey track between early arable growth.

Despite the season, the early risen sun is pleasantly warm on our backs. That same warmth will soon burn off the morning mist and fog. It is that sort of day, still within the throws of winter, that gently hints at the warmer and longer days of spring ahead.

After joining a metalled road winding its way through open fields for a time, we turn right up through the parkland, steadily rising. The tree-lined southern edge to the wood is in front, and the first few metres of woodland floor reveals itself to be densely carpeted by robust green bluebell shoots brought on by the warm February sunshine.

We enter the wood and make our way along woodland paths, before eventually ending up at Knobbly Knott, escorted briefly by bold chaffinches and the odd squirrel. Lingering long enough for a quick swing at the top, and without injury, we drop down the Knott's wooded western slope.

The warmth of the sun is lost as we move into shade. And with a hint of remnant fog hanging undisturbed between the countless trunks, the temperature drops jarringly. Zips are redone and hands thrust deep into pockets.

Before us, a dead straight grassy ride stretches out, tapering to a wooded point in the distance, interrupted here and there by substantial deadfalls of long-dead sweet chestnut. We negotiate tangles of branches and scramble up and over the fissured bark with care.

A solitary roe deer catches the old friend's eye about two hundred yards to our right, nearly lost against the backdrop of trunks and undergrowth. The doe stands still, the epitome of the wild – alert, muscles tensed ready for flight. She gives away no movement, remaining still, content to check our passing. We stop, and for a while, we share the same time and space, but we are visitors to her woodland refuge. Her attention is diverted away by something out of our sight, and we continue on, leaving the doe to blend perfectly with the trees and plants of her wood.

A little while later, and still with thoughts of the doe, we make our way along the southern edge. Shafts of diagonal sunlight punctuate the lifting mist and biblically illuminate the woodland floor here and there in sharp relief, beneath the dense fir canopy. We retrace our steps back to the wood edge and into open country.

This is the last entry before we venture fourth into the Spring Wood. In reality though, spring is already well underway with signs all-round of haste and vitality.

The Winter Wood is not quite over yet; later on in the year, as we near the end of this journal, we will re-enter the Winter Wood and if the fates allow, we will bring you further tales of frost, and maybe even snow, and of course Christmas rituals.

But, for now, it is about the spring, promising vibrant greens, kaleidoscope colours and renewed vigour.

PART TWO
SPRING WOOD

TEN

BEFORE THE STORM

Sunday, 3 March 2019 – 07.00

Newly named storm Freya is due to hit the Midlands later today, but for now there is a gentle breeze and steady drizzle, with little hint of the tempest to come.

We take the regular ancient route this morning along the main track and passing by the side of the archway. I am joined by the old friend this morning; it is becoming something of a habit – just like the old days, when we would regularly walk Ollie, my miniature schnauzer, and Alfie, the old friend's Staffordshire bull terrier up the wood. Rather fitting then this morning that we are also joined by Pippa, an eleven-year-old Staffordshire bull terrier crossed with a whippet – hard to visualise I know, but picture big teeth and lithe legs.

I think in the circumstances, now is the right time to share with you a bit about Ollie and his long-suffering friend, Alfie, both now sadly gone but fondly remembered. They were invariably up the wood together and loved it in different ways. For Ollie, the wood was an eager opportunity to explore, to go charging through undergrowth, somewhere out of sight and along some game trail, or around burrows and setts, nose to ground and ever alert but entirely impotent. For Alfie it was all about the swing on Knobbly Knott, or a log several sizes too big for him with which he would hamstring you. They were an unlikely pairing but inseparable. And even after five years apart, on reuniting on the return from New Zealand, there was an unmistakable recognition and a comfortable settling back into old ways.

Even now, it is still odd visiting the wood without either of them by our side.

The woodland floor is steadily becoming a carpet of green with the urgent growing of robust green bluebell shoots, breaking through the humus and leaf litter. The vibrant leaves of the understorey of young hawthorn and hazel are just starting to break bud. The honeysuckle leads the charge.

The days are gradually drawing out and after-work evening walks will soon be possible.

It appears Bran the raven may have found a partner. We come across the pair croaking gently to each other high up in the still bare canopies.

ELEVEN

OF THE KESTREL

Sunday, 10 March 2019 – 07.00

It is very windy this morning even before the storm – storm Gareth this time.

The daughter is back from university and joins me for today's visit. I am eager and excited to surprise her with the Brookside Lane route into the wood this morning. It will be her first time.

The woodland canopy, laid out before us and stretching to the horizon, remains winter bare, but Em is nevertheless impressed by this new landscape and vista – the wood seen from an altogether different perspective.

Em and I drop down the grassy slope of the pasture and enter the northern edge. In amongst the now constant carpet of countless thousands of bluebell shoots, other woodland plants are coming to life, breaking forth of the leaf litter and humus but not yet in flower. I have a couple to clumsily describe for you but only of the leaves for now; the flowers, we will describe at the appropriate time.

There are patches of the following woodland plant species dotted in clusters throughout the wood; the first is wood anemone (*Anemone nemorosa*); it grows close to the ground with feathery-like leaves of three lobes. The wood anemone is perennial and flowers between March and May. I remember Dad telling me that folk names for the wood anemone include 'thumbleweed' and 'smell fox'.

The next early plant and foreteller of spring is lesser celandine (*Ficaria verna*) also found in abundance throughout the wood. The lesser celandine has distinctive dark green heart-shaped leaves and grows to between seven and twenty centimetres in height. It is also perennial and flowers between March and May. The lesser celandine also goes by the name of 'pilewort', having been historically used to treat piles (probably best to stick to prescribed treatments).

There is a Flower, the Lesser Celandine,
That shrinks, like many more, from cold and rain;
And, the first moment that the sun may shine,
Bright as the sun himself, 'tis out again!

The Lesser Celandine (excerpt)
William Wordsworth

We shall see both of these plants in flower soon.

We wander the familiar winding pathways and speak of family matters and student life away from hearth and home. Eventually, Em and I find ourselves at the long, low, rambling patch of rhododendron where we also come across a mature patch of daffodils in full flower growing beside the path; they are a burst of welcome spring yellow standing proud in the green of the wood. Along with the rhododendron, the daffodils are perhaps another hint of curious domestication at this location in the depths of the wild wood far from settlement. There is a story to tell here I am sure, maybe even a secret long forgotten and passed out of memory. We shall never hear it, but it stirs the imagination.

We make our way back to the northern edge, passing young hawthorn and hazel in very early leaf. The just emerged hawthorn leaves, a delicate and luminous green – before their later waxy dark green appearance – are edible and have a delicate, slightly peppery flavour. The hawthorn also goes by the name of 'quickthorn' testament to its vigorous quick growth.

We leave the confines of the wood and head back to Brookside Lane. At the top of the slope out in the open, before we drop down towards the lane, we stop awhile and gaze, heads tilted upwards, at the small, neat, ever-vigilant kestrel, hovering, stationery on barely wimpling wings, while the west winds blow below and around him.

> *I caught this morning morning's minion, king-*
> *dom of daylight's dauphin, dapple-dawn-drawn Falcon,*
> *in his riding*
> *Of the rolling level underneath him steady air, and striding*
> *High there, how he hung upon the rein of a wimpling wing*
> *In his ecstasy! then off, off forth on swing,*
> *As a skate's heel sweeps smooth on a bow-bend: the hurl*
> *and gliding*
> *Rebuffed the big wind. My heart in hiding*
> *Stirred for a bird, – the achieve of, the mastery of the thing!*

The Windover (excerpt)
Gerard Manley Hopkins

TWELVE

AFTER THE STORMS

Sunday, 17 March 2019 – 07.30

Storm Freya and Gareth have passed and leave us with deep blue spring skies. It is cold this morning but without frost.

Pippa and the old friend join me again and we take the archway route and by all appearances have the wood to ourselves. We should enjoy it while we can; in four or so weeks' time, my wood will be a very busy place, although thankfully, only for a short while. We take the left-hand path off the main track and follow the northern edge, heading east. There is clear evidence of the storms in the form of the scatter of fallen branches on the path ahead.

A jay, not too far off but nevertheless out of sight to our left, marks our unwelcome intrusion with its jarring screech. A long time ago, on one of the camping trips in this northern part of the wood, my friends and I were disturbed in the dark, remote hours by the same screeching. It is not too difficult to imagine – at that young age, in the dark wild wood, and away from the comfort of your own bed – that the perfectly natural call of the jay is a sound far more sinister.

Leaving the jay's call behind, we wind our way along the northern edge, up through the high beeches and past the ancient, terraced sett before arriving at the five-bar gate. Out in the parkland, and some distance from the main flock in the distance, a solitary ewe lays cosily in amongst last year's bracken, chewing the cud, jaw moving in slow, deliberate, round motion. The ewe is serenely enfolded in a bright silver halo of startling white light.

Amongst the emerging new life all round us, we spot what must be the first and very early solitary bluebell flower; a portent of what will very soon be a dazzling display of purple wonder.

A little further on, on our way up Knobbly Knott, I spot the first couple of wood sorrel leaves coloured luminous vibrant green. Wood sorrel (*Oxalis*) is another woodland species lying in sometimes dense mats of distinctive three-leaf tiny plants. It has the appearance of clover but is quite different. Wood sorrel is edible and, when chewed between your front teeth, gives off a sharp, tangy taste, a lot like the tangy flavour of the Granny Smith apple. The taste is an unexpected surprise when measured against its otherwise regular clover-like appearance. You will notice that on occasion, the three leaves are folded down in readiness for the dark and just before rain.

On our way back to the arch, we catch a glimpse of a gorse clump in full flower up the bank beyond the woodland edge – it is a burst of spring gold against the green.

THIRTEEN

OF THE HUMBLE BEE

Sunday, 24 March 2019 – 07.20

It is chilly again this morning, but we set off under a welcome cloudless blue sky. There is no wind. The spring equinox has passed, and the lighter hours are ever so slightly longer than the nights. The canopies are still largely bare, but buds of all shapes and sizes are beginning to swell and stand ready. It is the last walk with Pippa for company this morning and the old friend is with me. We head past the arch and follow the time-worn track.

I am on the lookout this morning for new plants to discover and describe to you. Most are not yet in flower, making identification a little harder. The modern "apps" I have installed on our go-to phones are frankly not much use and are therefore not recommended. You cannot beat a good well-thumbed field guide equal to the task.

So, the first plant I spot, about two hundred yards or so in on the right-hand side of the main track is, I think, sweet woodruff (*Galium odoratum*). It is distinctive and easily (says me, with little confidence) set apart from the surrounding bluebell shoots (not yet in flower). Sweet woodruff has elliptical whorls of six to nine separate leaves arranged at the top of long, sinewy stems, looking a bit like a parasol. It is a perennial woodland plant – that is to say it returns every year. We shall hopefully see it in flower in a month or so's time. Sweet woodruff is a herb and has been used for medicinal purposes and as a flavouring in foods and beers. Beyond the sweet woodruff, and a little way off, a startled pheasant takes flight to our right, exploding from the cover of the woodland floor and in strenuous flight into the distance. I do not recall seeing a pheasant so deep within the wood before.

A little further on there are clumps of a plant with quite large arrow-shaped leaves with a wrinkly glossy finish. I am going to go out on a limb and propose that it is lords and ladies (*Arum maculatum* – what a lovely scientific name). It is another perennial and common in our woodlands. Growing to between fifteen and thirty-five centimetres in height, it will flower in April to May, when I will hopefully be able to confirm the species – it has a distinctive flower in the form of a yellow-green bract which unfurls to reveal a brown spike – I think it has an almost tropical appearance, quite distinct and exotic compared to our other native plant species hereabouts. Other names for lords and ladies include 'cuckoo pint' and 'naked girls and naked boys'. The name 'lords and ladies' allegedly stems from the resemblance of the flower to the male and female genitalia. A word of warning: the plant is poisonous, and the leaves should not be confused with those of common sorrel.

Out of habit, we pause briefly at the five-bar gate; the parkland is washed in spring sunshine and we watch for a while the crows and jackdaws playing in the oaks and foraging in the parkland.

We continue on and follow the southern edge where we spot a couple more very early bluebell flowers. A little further on, in amongst the beeches, a solitary bumble bee randomly scouts the woodland floor, in search of who knows what – possibly a suitable hole for raising a family. It is the first bee of the year up the wood. The 'bumble bee', is relatively modern, made famous perhaps by Beatrix Potter (*The Tale of Mrs Tittlemouse*). Prior to that, our forefathers would have commonly known them as 'humble bees', not because they are perceived as humble but simply because they hum in their seemingly erratic, directionless travels. It is a welcome further indicator of spring and new life.

Perhaps even older name for the bumble bee, or humble bee, is 'dumbledore', put to word by the hand of Thomas Hardy.

A shaded lamp and a waving blind,
And the beat of a clock from a distant floor:
On this scene enter – winged, horned, and
spined –
A longlegs, a moth, and a dumbledore;
While 'mid my page there idly stands
A sleepy fly, that rubs its hands…

Thus meet we five, in this still place,
At this point of time, at this point in space.
–My guests besmear my new-penned line,
Or bang at the lamp and fall supine.

"God's humblest, they!" I muse. Yet why?
They know Earth-secrets that know not I.

An August Midnight
Thomas Hardy

I am rather taken by the names 'humble bee' and 'dumbledore'.

We pass the shrine; new votive offerings lie purposefully placed or reverently hung from the lower branches, twisting lazily in the slight breeze.

A mature wild cherry high up to our left on the deer bank is breaking into bright white flower. Onwards, past the streams, we see the first wood anemone in delicate white flower, head bent and tightly closed this early morning. We pass a younger beech, breaking bud to reveal vibrant green new growth.

All around us are the unmistakable signs of spring.

We must mention the birds, as repetitive as that may be; the contact call of the tits and the song of the robin surrounds us, interrupted by the harsher call of the invisible crows.

FOURTEEN

OF THE OWL

I had one of those very rare special moments within the wood this evening. One that my clumsy hand cannot sufficiently convey to you. But I will try. It is Friday evening and rather than the normal pint with friends, I have decided upon an evening wood walk. I am joined by the new friend.

We park up at the greens and walk in via Brookside Lane which runs for a time alongside the young Nene – its banks dotted with primrose in full bright yellow flower against the otherwise dark brown of the bank – and then past the burial ground and allotments on the edge of the village. The late orange sun has gone down, but it is still light and before the gloaming.

We enter the northern edge and branch right, mostly just following our noses and lost in idle conversation. Inevitably, we end up at Knobbly Knott in the falling light. I hope to catch sight of the badgers, and so we lower our voices and tread more lightly. But we are either too early or too late, or maybe they remain abroad somewhere.

We pass a solitary primrose (*Primula vulgaris*), its yellow flowers bright in the half-light. I had thought that the primrose had been lost from the wood, presumably ravaged by those looking to transplant to their garden. But at least one remains. It was nice to see, and Dad would be pleased. The primrose is a perennial and at home in woodland. The uncultivated yellow white rosette of petals is unmistakeable. The primrose hails spring, being one of the earlier flowering spring plants, providing a source of food for early foraging bumble bees. All of the plant is edible; the leaves can be used for steeping to make wild tea and the flowers can be used to make wine. The primrose is however protected by legislation and consequently it is illegal to pick the flowers or disturb the plant. Another name for primrose is 'Butter rose' and in folklore, children who eat the primrose are said to be able to see the fairy folk.

We head down the northern side of Knobbly Knott and up to the southern edge of the wood, with the deer bank to our left. It is dusk now, in the silvery last light, and every trunk, branch and twig is silhouetted in vivid relief against the blue-black cloudless sky.

I hear the soulful call of the tawny owl off to our left, outside of the wood but nearby. I catch a swift silent shape flying on stealthy wings, and my eyes keep pace. I watch as the owl alights soundlessly on a branch above us and slightly to our left, just a dark shape and so close. He is silent for a short while and must know we are here, watching, although we keep quiet and remain still. He bares us no heed and begins calling again. There is a sense of haste and urgency in his call, a desire to get on with the business of spring. He does not keep us company for long, and we watch as he spreads his large, rounded wings and heads back out into open country, calling as he goes. I am rather more animated than my friend at the encounter. It is a rare moment, a memory that I know I will carry forever.

The remainder of the walk is mostly uneventful, apart from disturbing a night-time deer; it crashes with haste through the undergrowth and leaf litter somewhere ahead in the dark. We leave the wood in nearly full dark, with our tawny owl calling far off in the distance, returning to the greens via Chapel Lane. The cosy orange glow of The Windmill is inviting.

FIFTEEN

OF THE BUZZARD

Sunday, 7 April 2019 – early afternoon

Sometimes the wood can be reluctant to share its secrets; today is one of those days. Apart from the ever-present bird calls, the middle of the day is not the time for the wild. The wood is peaceful and still, at rest and a little sombre. Although, this is maybe a reflection of my own mood. The sky is overcast grey and there is no wind.

There can be no doubt that spring is well underway. The woodland floor is speckled with yellow and white flowers, and in places the green is giving way to the hint of a purple hue. Young hazel and beech are in vivid green leaf, and the honeysuckle and elder are nearly in full leaf. Wild cherry, common throughout the wood, blazes in white flower, if only for a short time, before the papery petals are scattered in flurries by the winds.

It is a short walk today, up to the five-bar gate and then left, up into the high beeches before heading back to the arch. On the way back, a section of the path which I have used for the last forty years or so is blocked by a fallen wild cherry still in flower. Already, a new path is forming, marked by the passage of humans and beasts alike. A diversion around the obstacle is clear on the woodland floor. The once well-walked path lying unused below the fallen trunk will soon succumb to the wild.

On the way back to the car, out in the open, I stop to watch an approaching buzzard from the north, up high, soaring effortlessly in graceful circles on unseen thermals on its lone journey. I watch for a while until the raptor is a black speck against the grey, high in the acres of sky over our wood.

SIXTEEN

OF THE DEER

The persistent cold of the last few days has given way to warm spring weather.

The past weekend was busy with returning Em to Sussex University and therefore no chance for a trip up the wood. But I am making up for it this midweek evening. I have purpose (not that I need an excuse) – the father-in-law has asked me to gather pine cones to finish off a bug hotel that he has been putting together for the local infant school, and he wants it finishing before the children return from their Easter break.

I am alone, and it is nice. Not that I do not welcome company, but sometimes a trip up the wood on the hunt and in lone contemplation is good for the mind and soul. Out of habit, I find myself at the long gone stand of horse chestnuts.

I have arrived at the same time as another couple with their dogs and I wonder what they must think of me alone, without a canine companion.

I make my way to the arch, between the freshly ploughed fields. It is warm and in the west the sun is shining, but the heavier approaching cloud to my left is brooding. We shall see. I know I mention it a lot, but I am struck by the myriad call of the birds from in the wood. From a distance, and as I approach, the song of all notes and pitches has an echoey, distant quality to it. And I am reminded of bird call-filled rain forests in the tropics seen on telly – our own woods and natural world are no less wonderful.

Today, whilst on site for work, I happened to find myself in a very small spinney of woodland sandwiched between a noisy road one side and suburbia the other. The floor of that remnant of wood – for that is what it must be – was covered by ramsons (wild garlic), not yet in flower. And, as we surveyed, the smell of garlic filled the air. I have never seen ramsons up my wood, but I am on the lookout tonight.

I pass to the side of the arch and turn right, skirting the southern edge and heading in an anticlockwise direction. The lower storey of trees – hazel, blackthorn, elder, quickthorn and young beech – are in vibrant green leaf, while the upper storey of the mature trees remains mostly bare. I am sure this is no accident and necessary for the younger trees to steel a march on their parents, before they 'green up' and cast deep shadow.

I think I have already mentioned that the young leaves of the quickthorn (hawthorn) can be foraged and eaten, but I am reminded now of a term my father-in-law uses at this time of year, when the hedgerows have that month or so period around April/May of bright, vibrant green growth. He refers to the appearance of the hedgerows and young quickthorn leaves at this time as 'bread and cheese'. I never remember my dad using the phrase and I am not entirely sure that my father-in-law knows the meaning. But, following a bit of research, it turns out that children used to gather young quickthorn and beech leaves for food and would refer to them as 'bread and cheese'. I have eaten both and they obviously taste nothing like bread and cheese, but that is not the point; in our modern world of convenience, we have forgotten what nature's wild larder has to offer, and I am sure, perhaps in hard times, such leaves would have been a rich source of essential vitamins and minerals.

I continue on, down through the babbling streams and then steadily upwards, following the western edge but a little way in from it. The wood floor now has a subtle purple hue, but the bluebells are not yet at their peak and with only a hint of perfume in the air. Another week, and especially with the four days of warm sunshine forecast ahead, the woods will be that signature blue and very busy (thankfully only for short while). I will tell you more about the lore of the bluebell then.

In amongst the subtle blue are white and yellow flowers in abundance. I have already described the white flower of the wood anemone to you. The other white flowers, seen throughout the woodland floor at the moment, are that of wood sorrel; the delicate ground-hugging plant has five bright white petals and yellow stamens. The early flowers hang their heads low like a bell, before unfurling later on. The yellow star-shaped flowers are that of the pretty lesser celandine; it has eight petals which have a glossy yellow finish. The flowers provide welcome relief amongst the green and are a comforting sign of spring.

I mention the streams with their flowing water, but the wood is noticeably dry, testament to the generally low rainfall. Normally around this time of year, as in the autumn and winter, wellies would be essential, but not for now.

As I head east, into the heart of the wood and on the approach to Knobbly Knott, I disturb three roe deer – three does with brown coats and bright white rumps. Perhaps yearlings. They take flight two hundred or so yards to my right, but then stop, alert and watchful. We stand, us four, and look upon each other for a while, them at home and me the interloper. But they do not move on, content to know that I am here, within sight and just far enough away. Relaxed enough to return to grazing the bright and lush woodland grass. I decide to try and make my way a little closer, using a thicket of holly as cover between me and them. And, whilst I close in by seventy yards or so, they are no fools, and as I emerge from the side of the holly, I watch as they bound gracefully away.

Another special moment and precisely why I am here.

In pursuit of the deer, I am off the path now and tread carefully between the bluebell plants.

Remaining off the path and in making my way generally in the direction of the Knott, I come across another surprise. I like to think that I know the wood as well as anywhere, but it still has secrets to share; I have stumbled across the remnants of ancient machinery – a twisted and rusted frame, broken and on its side, its base bedded in and covered by new growth. And just beside it, purposefully propped up against a sycamore trunk, there is a toothed steel wheel which must be nearly five feet in diameter. As you know, I am in at least my fortieth year up the wood, but I have never seen this before. What is it, and why is it here? I can only guess that it might be all that remains of a piece of ancient lumber equipment. There is always a story to tell.

Pondering on what the machinery was used for – and why it is here and how I have never seen it before – I arrive at the eastern edge and in amongst the conifers, where I take the opportunity to forage for pine cones of all different shapes and sizes. With the bag bursting at the seams, and a few spots of light rain which come to nothing, I continue on alone along the northern edge.

The late sun is a deep orange disk shrouded by the thin, low cloud in front of me and glimpsed between the trunks at the woodland edge. By the time I emerge, he has gone from orange to a perfect shrouded white disc, suspended a little way above the horizon.

A final note for this entry. I was wrong about the primrose – I just wasn't looking hard enough before; I spotted at least four other patches of bright yellow primrose this evening, in addition to the solitary plant mentioned a couple of entries ago.

No ramsons though.

And the bells of Badby church, normally wrung for practice on Wednesday nights and heard in the western part of the wood in the evening, are silent, it being Easter and all.

SEVENTEEN

OF THE CUCKOO

Good Friday, 19 April 2019 – 06.00

The gateway to the long weekend promises to be sunny and warm. I am up with the lark as they say, but no lark to be heard this morning. It is already light and at sunrise. Long wisps of cirrus cloud streak the blue, stretching out beyond the expanse ahead.

As I set out this early morning, I could not suspect that the wood had a great secret to reveal, one of the best.

I find myself on the east-west path traversing the wood and on the way up to the Knott. I am accompanied by spring bird call at the finale of the dawn chorus.

Spring flowers grow in number. Yellows and whites abound in amongst vibrant shades of green.

As the path starts to steadily rise to the summit, a familiar, but yet nearly forgotten and rare sound is carried through the trunks. It is the solitary call of the cuckoo heralding spring. Not just one call but many at regular intervals. The cuckoo is away somewhere to my left, to the south-west, perhaps even beyond the wood edge. It is hard to tell.

I stop to listen, to make the best of the moment. It has been too long since I last heard the cuckoo in the environs of the wood. It does not mean that they have not been present, but just that I have not been in the right place at the right time. For me, the call is the quintessential sound of the English countryside, even though they are only a brief visitor to our shores.

The call of the cuckoo would also stop Dad still in his tracks on the woodland path, imploring us youngsters to 'be quiet and listen', while we shuffled impatiently, not quite appreciating what all the fuss was about. All while he would just enjoy, chin raised, eyes searching, an appreciative smile lifting the corners of his mouth. I did not realise then just what a precious sound it is, but I do now of course, so rare it is.

The shape and plumage of the cuckoo looks something like a cross between a pigeon and perhaps a sparrowhawk. The upper plumage is slate grey, with barred sandy and dark plumage to the chest and dark grey colour to the wings and tail. The most well-known attribute of the cuckoo is its parasitisation of other bird nests, leaving the unsuspecting parents to raise the fledged cuckoo as if it were their own.

I wonder how long it will be before I hear the unforgettable 'cuckoo' again.

EIGHTEEN

OF CLOSE ENCOUNTERS

Easter Sunday, 21 April 2019 – 20.10

Sunday evening, after sunset.

The visit this evening is to bring you news of the badgers, but as nearly always, the wood and Mother Nature have other plans for me. I have chosen to visit the eastern sett, near to the south-eastern corner. The wind favours an approach from the west, so I head up the main track in the direction of the five-bar gate. Hopefully, I have the time just right and should arrive at the sett as twilight sets in. Right now, it is still mostly light, and all-round, the woodland floor is tinted blue in the failing light.

It is not long before I disturb a roe deer about fifty yards or so to my left. I catch only a glimpse of a solitary white rump urgently bounding off deeper into the wood and the encroaching twilight.

The wood is quiet, coming to rest and there is no wind. Just the odd warning call of a blackbird far off in the distance. Every now and then, either side of the track, I hear the movement of the smaller beasts of the wood. Small, scurrying things unseen, hidden below dense, tangled vegetation. This is their time for foraging and protecting territory. But they must be ever vigilant for the owl on silent wings is abroad, calling somewhere to my right.

After ten minutes or so, I arrive at the five-bar gate and turn left. Now is the time for stealth; the sett is only four hundred yards or so away, so I make my way slowly up the slope on the approach, treading lightly and taking care to avoid fallen twigs. It is dusk, and just off the path either side, the wood is retreating to vague, dark shapes. A very gentle breeze is blowing but from the right direction and I remain downwind as I had hoped.

Five minutes more and I arrive close to the sett, just down the slope in front of me. But its openings and terraces are quiet at least for now. I sit down for the vigil, cross-legged on the dry, hardpacked earthen path and wait. All around me are the sounds of the night-time wood; crows and jackdaws bidding goodnight, a buzzard mewing far off beyond the wood and the din of anxious ewes calling for wayward playful offspring. There are other sounds less identifiable out there in the dark – clicks and knocks and rustlings that stir the imagination. As I sit, the wind changes direction ever so slightly, and I quietly adjust my position to remain downwind.

I wait patiently, but the sett is quiet and there is very little light left. There is a distinct snuffling noise off to my left, a way away down the slope out of sight that could be a badger, but it is intermittent and whatever it is does not draw nearer. I can only guess. Time passes and it gets darker still. I catch a glimpse of a fast-moving silhouetted black shape up in the canopies where it is a little lighter. It can only be the silent flight of an early emerged bat. It is sufficiently warm enough for it to have awoken from its winter torpor.

More time passes and I have given up hope, and as I am just about to move off, I have an encounter; a bat, perhaps *the* bat, flies directly at me at head height while I sit, within inches of my face. I do not see it, but it is close enough for me to hear the flap of its membraned leathery wings very close and to feel the disturbed air of its abrupt change in direction wash lightly over my face. Thankfully, I have no hair for a tangle to occur. And rather than feel perturbed, I am left smiling at the close encounter. I wonder who was more surprised?

So, I bring you news of the bat, and the badger's tale will have to wait for another time.

I head off in the dark and eventually arrive at the arch – its crenelated parapet is silhouetted against the last remnant of the day's light. And flanked by the dark of its stone abutments, and the trunks either side, the very last of the day's light above the horizon of the hills in the distance is framed by the arched opening.

NINETEEN

OF THE BLUEBELL

Sunday, 28 April 2019 – 15.00

In anticipation of a busier wood today, my youngest and I park up at the pleasant chestnut-dotted expanse of well-tended village greens and take the lesser used Brookside Lane route in. The spring sunshine is pleasant and warm. That first touch of proper spring warmth that is more than just skin deep and which truly signals the end of the dark months.

I mentioned recently of the hunt for ramsons (*Allium ursinum*), and whilst I am sure there are none in the wood itself, to my surprise we come across a small patch growing on the bank beside the very narrow path leading up to the ornate metal kissing gate. The dark green waxy leaves, long, bent over and tapering, and in a dense mat, have a distinct garlic smell –

hence ramsons' other name of 'wild garlic'. Both the leaves and flowers are edible. I am excited by this new find.

We pass through the kissing gate and head up the slope before emerging onto the upper pasture. The swathe of green grassland is speckled with dandelions in fine yellow flower. I have mentioned the lofty view of the wood from this spot before; last time, the canopies were bare, but now drab browns have given way to spring greens of all different hues. There is still the odd bare patch of trunk and branch, and I suspect I know the culprit. We shall see.

As we draw nearer the wood, we can see that the sycamores, beech and oaks are indeed in new leaf, but the lone budded ash remains skeletal. I am reminded of an old adage:

If the oak is out before the ash, we shall surely have a splash,
If the ash is out before oak, we shall surely have a soak.

It looks like we may be in for a dry year.

We enter the wood and into a world of blue wonder. For that is what the trip today is mainly about; in every direction, beneath the canopies, alongside the narrow pathways and between the trunks, there is a nearly unbroken carpet of blue. Not an inch of the woodland floor is spared. I am of course talking about the common bluebell (*Hyacinthoides non-scripta*) and hopefully the native variety. It is a sight to behold and a marker of my year, for many years.

The bluebell barely needs a description, but the clue is in the name; the purply blue flowers rise on one side of a green cylindrical stem twenty to twenty-five centimetres high, bending their frilly bell-like heads. And in such profusion, and as an accompaniment to their beauty, the air is filled with their fragrant sweet perfume. If you only go to the wood once a year, do so at this time, at the end of April. You will not be disappointed. But enjoy them where they belong; do not attempt to pick them, for bluebells brought across the threshold into the home is bad luck. Aside from simply enjoying their grace, their only other use I know is that their white bulbs can be mashed to release the starch and sugars to make an effective glue.

Whilst the wood is famous for the bluebell and just deserved, and while the flowers of wood anemone, celandine and wood sorrel have gone over, since my last full daylight trip, there are many other woodland flowers gracing the woodland floor at the moment that are equally worthy of mention.

As we enter the northern edge, in amongst the blue there are large swathes of the dazzling white flower of the greater stitchwort (*Stellaria holostea*); the round-ended flowers appear to have ten petals, but they actually have five, with each petal having a deep central notch, making it easily identifiable. The flowers are about one to two centimetres across. The leaves too, arranged in opposing pairs up the slender, tall stem are distinctive, being long and narrow like a spearhead. Greater stitchwort flowers between April and May and has a great many local names – one of them I rather like is 'Daddy's shirt buttons'. The name 'stitchwort' appears to derive from the use of the plant in herb lore to cure the painful stitch that we all remember from tiresome and arduous cross-country runs at school.

As we move on, we pass a plant that looks a little like a nettle but with a yellow flower. I have always assumed it to be a type of dead nettle but with yellow flowers, rather than white or red. It transpires that it is actually yellow archangel (*Lamium galeobdolon*), and it does look very much like the nettle, with large, triangular, tooth-edged leaves on the lower part of the stem, growing smaller in size towards the top of the upright stem. The bright yellow flowers have an orchid appearance, with three-pronged lower parts etched with red lines, topped by a yellow hood. The flowers grow close to the stem in a whorl and at regular intervals between the leaves. Yellow archangel grows to a height of around thirty-forty centimetres and flowers between April and June. Fear not, it is not a nettle and so will not sting you. It has been suggested that the name 'archangel' derives from the absence of the sting.

When I was a kid, a trip up the wood with Dad to see the bluebells was met with a challenge; there was a promise of fifty new pence for the first of us to spot a rogue whitebell amongst all their blue sisters. But the whitebells are few and far between. I have carried the tradition on with my three and so Jim Bob is on the hunt for the whitebell this afternoon. Thankfully, low inflation being what it is, I think a fifty pence piece is still fair reward.

We continue on through the Spring Wood, generally heading west. Wandering and happy, pondering the latest of Jim's harebrained ideas. But it is pleasant, and I listen, without really listening. I want to show her the ancient, rusted metalwork discovered recently and so we head in that direction. After a bit of a search, and treading carefully through the bluebells, I show her the intriguing, twisted frame and giant cogged wheel.

We skirt Knobbly Knott and stick to the lesser used paths, seeking to avoid the myriad of human activity, busy brandishing tripods and the like. We take one such lesser path, clear between the green and blue but covered in undisturbed leaf litter. We clamber over a couple of deadfalls before the path finally peters out, lost in the tangle of undergrowth, preventing further easy passage. But it is not completely wasted time, as on the way back, Imogen spots a single perfect whitebell in amongst all its blue sisters. And I am fifty pence poorer.

After a time, we arrive at the five-bar gate and take the main track heading in the direction of the arch. I have my eye in now, and there are more plants and flowers to describe for you.

There is a tallish plant with a white flower. I identify it as garlic mustard (*Alliaria petiolata*). It has large, triangular, toothed-edged leaves that descend in size up the stem. The leaves are not dissimilar in shape to a sycamore or acer leaf but a good deal smaller. It is a tall plant, at least noticeably taller than others around it, growing to between forty and 120 centimetres in height. The examples in the wood are around forty to fifty centimetres high. The stem is topped by a cluster of small white flowers, of four neat petals, each flower arranged in the shape of a cross. The leaves, when rubbed or crushed, have a garlic smell, and as with ramsons, can be used as a flavouring in food. British folklore names for garlic mustard include, 'sauce alone' and 'Jack-by-the-hedge'. Along with culinary uses, garlic mustard has been used to treat wounds.

Avoiding a throng of walkers trailing noisy children greedily clutching handfuls of terminal bluebells, and knowing that we must head west, we diverge off the main track, seeking solace, and continue on the hunt for new flowers.

Deep down, in amongst all the other growth of the woodland floor, including the greater stitchwort, is the very pretty purple blue flower of the common dog violet (*Viola riviniana*). Standing just a few centimetres above the humus, it is a beautiful, delicate flower with two lobed petals at the top and three lobes at the bottom. The leaves, arranged around the base of the plant, are distinctly heart shaped. Common dog violet goes by the other name of 'wood violet'.

Only a few metres further on, we spot another blue flower, this time named simply: 'bugle' (*Ajuga reptans*). Standing around thirty centimetres tall, the flowers and leaves are arranged in alternate order up the hairy square stem, again in descending size towards the tip (presumably to maximise the light). The leaves of the bugle are oval shaped with smooth edges and shiny, with pronounced 'pillowey'-like bumps over their shiny surface. The flowers, purply blue in colour, comprise of a single petal shaped a bit like a lady in a dress but I suppose if you want to be technical, one large lower lobe flanked by two smaller upper lobes, arms outstretched and welcoming. The petal has distinct deeper blue lines within the centre of each lobe, fading to lighter blue. Bugle also goes by the name of 'carpenter's herb' testament to the use of the plant to stem bleeding from a cut.

And finally for today, the last plant we spot is bush vetch (*Vicia sepium*). The most distinctive part of the plant is its leaves which are arranged alternately on stems off the main square stem. Each secondary stem has up to sixteen separate alternate tear-shaped leaves, dark green in colour and with a pronounced central vein running the length of the leaf from tip to base. The purple flowers are small and packed in tight clusters up the stem, comprising of a trumpet terminating in four lobes – two side by side at the bottom and two branching out to the side above. Bush vetch grows to between twenty and sixty centimetres in height and flowers in May to October.

Apologies for the length of the entry today, but I think it was worth it, wasn't it? After all, I want to bring you descriptions of the plants that call the wood home and which are suggestive of its ancient age and diversity. Anyway, we leave her embrace where we entered, but just before we go, and on the very edge of the wood, I spot the industrious activity of a thrush; broken snail shells of striped browns and creamy yellows lay ruined and scattered on top of and about a handy flat stone, just beside the path. I have mentioned before that the thrush is a rare sight, but they are clearly about.

TWENTY

OF THE BADGER

We are on the hunt for the badger – again. We park up after sundown and head for the arch. We are greeted with a glorious sunset; the ragged clouds to our right – the remnants of storm Hannah – are lit up by fiery oranges and reds by the dying sun on its measured descent below the western horizon. We have the wood to ourselves, or so it seems.

As we approach the northern edge, a solitary roe deer takes flight from a grassy hollow about a hundred yards to our left and melts effortlessly into the cover and safety of her wood. With the wind very lightly blowing from the south, we head right, skirting the northern edge with a view to arriving at our destination downwind of the sett. I have chosen the middle sett tonight, lying at the base of Knobbly Knott. We are a bit early and so take our time, treading lightly and in hushed tones, just enjoying the silence of the wood.

Imogen stops every now and then to snap a shot of a posing perfect bluebell. The wood has a healthy, honest, earthy smell this evening following the rains. After fifteen minutes or so we make our way carefully up the long, northern slope of the Knott and take care to remain downwind. Near to the top, an exposed buttress root of an ancient beech makes a handy, if not hard and lumpy seat.

And we wait in patient anticipation.

While the light fades to silvery tones and silhouettes, we are serenaded in the gloaming by a male and female tawny owl, calling to each other in the leafy treetops close by, the screech of the female contrasting with the softer, flute-like hoot of the male. We are about thirty or so yards from the sett, which is away down the slope, and have a view of its openings, marked by a slightly darker point against the slightly lighter background. We are losing the light fast now, and definition is falling all-round, individual trunks coalescing to form upright black masses as the dark creeps in. I catch a tantalising glimpse of silent movement from around the sett, but it is fleeting and gone.

Minutes pass, and then, from the far side of a pronounced mound, the opening hidden from view, a white-striped badger emerges, and then is quickly followed by another, but as soon as they are seen, they are gone, wasting no time and heading out into the expanse of the wood on the hunt for earthworms and other such oozy woodland morsels. I am confident that the badgers are unaware of our presence, so we remain seated, bottoms growing steadily numb, despite stealthy shuffling to avoid the worst of gnarly protrusions.

More minutes pass and still we sit hunched – patient, hushed and quiet.

And to our right, down the slope, the two badgers come back into view in urgent shambling gait, bolting down their sett out of sight and into safe earthen refuge. I am perplexed as to what could have caused them to run – or rather – shamble so quickly for cover. But, soon after, we hear unguarded voices from the same direction and the silhouettes of a couple come into view; they may be interested in more than just the wildlife.

So, with our vigil brought to a premature end, and in near darkness, we head out away from the Knott, bidding the strangers goodnight. But I am not disappointed. Even a brief glimpse of the secretive brock at home, in their wood, is enough.

And no bat!

TWENTY-ONE
OF THE BEES

Sunday, 12 May 2019 – 11.15

The walk in via the greens and Brookside Lane is becoming something of a comfortable habit – it is away from the throng, and it is intimate. I am straying from the subject of the wood a little now but cannot resist describing new discoveries for you. On the opposite bank of the young Nene flanking the lane, and in the shade of towering oak and beech, is a long swathe of ramsons. I had not spotted them before, in amongst the other growth, but they are in full flower now, in the sunshine – a burst of bright white sparks. On my left-hand side, in the dappled shade of the hedge, a single lords and ladies flower stands out from the ivy-covered ground, tropical and alien. It is a reminder for me to check to see if the lords and ladies I thought I had spotted a few entries ago in the wood is yet in flower.

And out in the meadow, in the shade of the wood edge, there is a pink flower in amongst the lush grass; I think it is cuckooflower (*Cardamine pratensis*), comprising of four round, lobed petals, lilac in colour with a yellow-green centre. Its rounded leaves are arranged along the stem in ladder fashion. The cuckooflower is sacred to the unseen fairy folk, so pick at your peril!

I enter the cool of the wood through its now leafy northern edge.

The first thing I notice is the bluebell; we still have the blue, but it has lost its lustre, and it is a lighter, paler blue. The previously arched slender leaves of the bluebell lay flat against the woodland floor now and their dark green appearance is fading to tired limes and yellows. The result of all of this is the woodland floor has a slightly tired look, but it is only for a brief time. And it is with the comforting knowledge that in a year from now we shall have that same blue wonder all over again. Already though, other new growth can be seen over the woodland floor; bracken plants – broken out from the curled fiddleheads we observed earlier – now stand up in ascendency above the fading bluebells. Everywhere you look, you can see the bracken, and whilst it is a picture, I am left wondering how healthy it is.

I wander to the western part of the wood amongst the constant, distant chatter of other visitors. But mixed in and another sign of spring, edging slowly towards summer, is the drone of insects above my head in the ever-expanding canopy. The woodpeckers are busy today as well; there are two nearby, hammering away at trunks in search of sustenance. And as an accompaniment to the woodpecker, Bran and his partner croak to each other, out of sight. What do they speak of, I wonder, in their corvid language?

I find myself (by design) at the long stand of rhododendron to check on the progress of the flowers. The swollen teardrop rhododendron buds are just starting to break, revealing cracks of deep purple flower hidden within; another week or so and this large spread of invasive plant will be in full flower.

I think I have said before that the rhododendron sits by the side of a clearing in the canopies (the frost pocket mentioned back in the winter); today it is bathed in sunshine, and I stop awhile to watch two butterflies dancing with each other, in their erratic, seemingly directionless flight. I try and keep pace, waiting for them to alight long enough so that I can take a photo for identification, but they are a tease, fluttering on each time I draw closer (what a sight I must be for the observer). But perseverance eventually pays off; the first butterfly is largely white (smaller than a cabbage white) and with grey-black markings at its wing tips. Its partner, the same size, is also white but has bright yellow patches on its wings, fading to orange and then brown at the wing edge. I wonder whether they are the male and female of the same species?

But upon returning home, armed with the photographs I have taken, I decide that the first is a wood white, according to my field guide. Like me I suppose, they are a haunter of the wood, preferring woodland clearings for food and mating. The second, I think is the orange tip (again according to the guide) and likely not a mate to the wood white after all. Confirmation is provided by the green mottled underside of the wings I have captured in one of my photographs. The orange tip is also at home in the wood but equally frequents hedgerows and the woodland edge. So, not mates after all. They nevertheless show great interest in each other. I move on at the sound of approaching visitors and leave the butterflies to their graceful aerial ballet.

I am again on the lookout for spring flowers so that I can bring you a complete record. It is only when you really start to intentionally look that, in addition to the recognisable flowers that you take for granted, there are many others equally worth a mention. I have seven to describe for you today, all found in my wanderings and spotted from the pathways.

We are all familiar with what I know, and have always known, as 'stickyweed' (*Galium aparine*). It is a perennial plant that can be found in abundance nearly everywhere you look, including in the wood. It grows in sinewy sticky curtains using other plants for support and can, because of this, reach good height, smothering the hapless plants beneath. The stems, along with the whorls of narrow leaves spaced at regular intervals along its length, are covered in tiny hooks, visible only with a magnifying glass. It is the effective and efficient hooks that give the impression of 'stickyness' and enable pranks to be played on unsuspecting friends. The plant is a nuisance for dog owners; I have spent too much time picking the equally sticky seeds out of the hair of an impatient and wriggling Oliver (no more, sadly).

I did not know, but the proper name for stickyweed is 'cleavers'. Another name is 'robin-run-the-hedge' – what a lovely name! It is fair to say that stickyweed does not bring a great deal to the party flower-wise, but they are there, sited where the leaves meet the stem. The flowers are tiny, no more than a couple of millimetres across, and are white with a green centre.

I have known for a long time that stickyweed is edible, but it needs to be boiled or steamed to disarm the unpalatable hooks. And apparently, the seeds can be roasted and ground for a coffee substitute (although I would imagine it must be a very labour-intensive foraging exercise for a single cup!). The plant is probably best left for sticking to friends' jumpers.

In amongst the fading blue, and the white of the greater stitchwort, there are purples and reds.

Herb Robert (*Geranium robertianum*), dotted throughout the wood, has a purply pink flower comprising five petals up to two centimetres across; the petals are a deeper colour at their edges, fading to a lighter pink-purple in the middle. Each petal has two distinct deeper purple stripes arranged lengthways, making it easily identifiable. The leaves of herb Robert are triform in shape, with each of the three joined leaves having deep lobes. The stems of the plant are noticeably hairy. The examples of herb Robert in the wood are around twenty to thirty centimetres in height. It flowers from May to September and is an annual/biennial, relying on seed distribution for establishing the next generation. Another name for herb Robert is, rather darkly, 'death come quickly'.

The next flower I spot is that of the red campion (*Silene dioica*). The flowers are a uniform purply pink two centimetres across, and each of its five petals are deeply notched. I think they have a slightly ragged, unkempt appearance. The leaves are a long oval shape and arranged in pairs up each hairy stem. The woody brown seed pods of red campion are noticeable later on in the year, having the appearance of a woody goblet. Red campion is a perennial and flowers from May to August.

A little further on there are yellow flowers to be seen – that of the buttercup (*Ranunculus repens*). It transpires that there are three common British buttercup species, but I think this example is the creeping buttercup, which prefers damp conditions. Nearby, there is another smaller yellow flower whose stems appear to grow along the ground rather than upwards. It has five petals, with each petal ending in a slight point, and the leaves are oval shaped. This one has me foxed; it is not St John's wort – the leaves are the wrong shape, and the flower does not have the noticeable stamens seen in the photographs of the flower in the guidebooks. And it is not marsh marigold – the flower is very similar, but the leaves are very different. So, for now, it will have to remain nameless, and I will update you if and when I can.

The final flower for today is germander speedwell (*Veronica chamaedrys*); it is a pretty little blue flower, no more than a centimetre across and comprising four petals. The top petal and those each side are about the same size, but the bottom petal is much smaller, giving the flower an uneven, asymmetrical appearance. The petals are strikingly bright blue, fading to light blue at the very edges. Deeper blue stripes run front to back on each petal. The middle of the flower is white with a green centre. The leaves are triangular shaped with soft teeth around the edge and are arranged in opposing pairs along the hairy stem. Germander speedwell is a perennial, flowering from March to July. The plant has been used for the brewing of tea and for the treatment of gout.

I make my way past the western edge of Knobbly Knott and arrive at the Great Beech; its hollowed out shady stump is occupied by bracken and a juvenile sycamore. I head up the slope, between the dense bramble to the nearby gateway at the very southern edge and lean for a time, looking out over the parkland and enjoying the warm sunshine on my upturned face. The Dower House sits hazy in the distance.

There is a gentle breeze stirring the leaves of the foliage away off to my left, generating a soft hiss which, somehow, does not sound quite right. The hiss grows by steady degrees and can no longer be the breeze. Instead, the air is filled with an unmistakeable hum, and I watch as a large swarm of bees flies along the southern edge and towards me; thirty thousand or so bees fill the air on the trail of their queen. In their hundreds, they pass over and around me, and I watch as they leave the open and head into the wood, but they do not move on, instead showing great interest in a dark vertical scar on the trunk of the sister to the Great Beech, around twenty feet or so above the ground, where I suspect their queen must have settled. I make my way back down to the stump and sit and watch the swarm awhile, mesmerised by their airborne dance.

I will admit to a very brief moment of panic as the bees approached and filled the air around me, but they cared not that I was there; I presented no threat. I am exhilarated and must confess, as soft as it sounds, that the moment is nearly spiritual. Another moment that I know I will not forget.

On the way back, I check on the lords and ladies on the western side of the main track on the way to the arch and find it just unfurling. It should be in full unusual flower next week.

I leave the wood with thoughts of the bees and their queen, and about how, just when I think I am struggling for inspiration for this journal, the wood's story is far from finished.

TWENTY-TWO

SILVER ON THE TREE

Wednesday, 15 May 2019 – 09.00

Now that the trees are in leaf (although the ash still has some catching up to do), it is my intention to tell you a bit about the trees that make up my wood – not all in one go, but over the coming weeks and months. I am going to start with the hawthorn, given that it is May and all.

Strictly speaking, whilst there is young hawthorn in the wood, no doubt self-set from defecating blackbirds and rather weedy and pathetic in appearance, there are no mature examples that I know of, but there are examples out in the parkland seen from the woodland edge, where they have the benefit of full sun and space.

There is a hawthorn visible from the five-bar gate at the end of the main track, seen through the sentinel oaks now in leaf, and it is in full flower – bright white silver covering every thorny bough. The hawthorn is one of my favourite trees and at this time of year it is a blaze of bright white and sometimes red, heralding full spring.

It is not the earliest flower in the hedgerow, blackthorn has that accolade, but it is the flower that normally signals the end of frosts and cold weather and the gateway to the warmer months.

I did not know, but locally, by that I mean the Midlands, there are two types of hawthorn: common hawthorn (*Crataegus monogyna*) and midland hawthorn (*Crataegus laevigata*). As far as I can see, the main differences are in the foliage and size of the plant. In the right circumstances, common hawthorn can grow to the size of a small tree whereas midland hawthorn grows to around the size of a large shrub. The leaves of the common hawthorn are deeply lobed, in three segments and around four to five centimetres in length. The leaves of midland hawthorn have noticeably more rounded lobes, three in number, edged in saw teeth. The leaves of both plants emerge supple and luminous green in the spring, before changing to a dark green with a rougher feel as spring gives way to summer.

A noticeable feature of hawthorn is the densely packed formation of the branches and defensive thorns – anyone who has ever had to struggle through a thick hawthorn hedge to retrieve a ball will know just how effective the thorns can be!

Hawthorn comes into flower around the second week in May. Common hawthorn only flowers in white, but midland hawthorn flowers in either white or pinky red. The flowers die down late May/June, and the fruit – known as haws – which ripen between August and October, are ruby red, darkening to maroon and slightly smaller than a pea in size. The hawthorn goes by other names including 'May tree' – the month in which the plant flowers.

Both the leaves and haws of the hawthorn are edible. I mentioned in an earlier entry that the young leaves of the hawthorn, when they are still soft and supple, are edible and have a green, slightly peppery taste. I guess along with 'Jack-by-the-hedge' (garlic mustard) and wood sorrel, they could be mixed to make a tasty wild salad.

I have foraged in the hedgerows for the haws in late summer/early autumn to make fruit jerky. If you are interested in making your own jerky, gather a good quantity of haws (around a pound or two) into a bowl and, using your thumb and index finger, squeeze the soft yellowy orange flesh out from the tough skin. With the de-skinned flesh in the bowl, kneed and squeeze the flesh into a thick paste. You will notice that the flesh quickly turns a rather unappetising orangery brown, but do not be put off. Feel free to pick out the inevitable and unmistakeable pale-coloured grubs (or leave in for a protein boost). Spread the viscous paste into a layer about half to one centimetre thick and either allow to air dry or, if you are impatient (as I am), place in the oven on a very low heat to speed up the drying. Test the firmness of the jerky and once it has little or no spring, it is ready for cutting into strips. The jerky has a fruity, tangy flavour and is highly recommended – it really is very good. And, once dried, the jerky lasts for ages.

A bit about the folklore of the hawthorn now. Robert Graves, the poet, mentions in his book *The White Goddess* the association of the hawthorn with Joseph of Arimathea's staff and the Crown of Thorns. In Gaelic folklore, the hawthorn has a strong association with the fairies. To cut down the hawthorn is to attract the unwanted attention of the fairies! You have been warned.

TWENTY-THREE
OF THE MINING BEE

Monday, 20 May 2019 – 11.00

Brookside Lane is becoming something of a habit. We make our way up to the upper pasture, past the ramsons still in flower in the shade of the yews overhanging the narrow path.

The dandelions have gone to seed, and the pasture is full of dandelion clocks, waiting for the wind to disperse the little parachutes far and wide. But the pasture is still full of yellow, and this time it is the buttercup. And in amongst the buttercups there are patches of the brilliant blue of germander speedwell.

Upon entering the wood, Jim and I spot a thrush, with its distinctive speckled chest and brown plumage. It has been a long time since I have seen a thrush in the wood, and I wonder if it has a brood nearby. I move into the undergrowth off the path, treading carefully so as to not trample the white swathes of stitchwort. I spot a slightly darker mass in a tangle of hazel and honeysuckle, around head height, and it is a nest – blackbird or thrush – but it is empty and of some age.

On our way to check on the rhododendron, we come across a tiny green caterpillar dangling precariously on a nearly invisible silk thread attached to the leafy canopy of the oak above us. I wonder what moth or butterfly it belongs to? The rhododendrons are speckled with pink, but they are not yet in full flower.

Our normal tranquil glade is a cacophony of blackbird alarm call this morning and not just one; there is a pair going at it and my suspicion is aroused. Near to the source of the noise, we spot at least two squirrels negotiating the twisted, interweaving branches of the rhododendron, and I wonder if the squirrels are the reason for the cacophony. I suspect that the squirrels may have spotted the blackbirds' nest and are after the eggs, or perhaps even the fledglings.

We make our way away from the din and leave nature to its own devices.

Our next port of call is a large plant that I have been keeping my eye on for a few weeks. It is tall and already as high as my waste. The leaves of the plant are arranged in opposing pairs and are oval shaped with a wrinkly surface and with sawtoothed edges. The plant terminates in yet to open buds. I suspect, because of its height and large sawtoothed leaves, that it is common figwort, but I will not definitely know until the plant flowers. It is one to keep an eye on.

Just a little way up the path, between the advancing bracken, we spot perfectly round uniform small burrows in the earth path. The tiny burrows, no more than half a centimetre across, are surrounded by slightly lighter mounds of excavated soil, clearly the industrious actions of a minibeast. A little further on, and for my first time, we spy the culprit. We are down on our hands and knees and see the reddy brown furry head of a bee just visible inside the burrow. In attempting to take a photo, and getting a little too close, the bee quickly retreats back into the darkness and refuge of its burrow, letting out a very brief buzz by way of warning. Retreating ourselves a little too, we watch as she re-emerges, her red-brown head clearly visible.

Upon returning home, and after a bit of research, I decide that it is a mining bee – a solitary bee, unlike our friends in the Great Beech. The hole in the woodland path is her burrow, excavated to lay her eggs, where her grubs will develop, feeding on pollen and honey provided by Mum. I have seen and wondered about the neat little holes for a long time, but it is the first time I have seen the occupant in action.

At the base of a bramble, we spot what I know to be cuckoo spit. It looks like a globule of frothy white bubbles that really do look like spit. This particular globule is nestled in-between the diverging stems of the bramble. It is not actually cuckoo spit at all, and honestly, the truth is a little more unsettling. The 'spit' is actually a result of the actions of the nymph of the cuckoo spit insect or frog hopper as I know it to be. The spit is discharged from the anus of the nymph and is precisely why I think I prefer it being the spit of the cuckoo. Slightly less revolting. You will have probably seen the insect; it is not much more than five millimetres long, is pale green in colour (there may be other varieties) and hops away, seemingly into thin air, when disturbed.

Close to the western base of Knobbly Knott, we spot another caterpillar, this time brown in colour. It is abseiling down from a branch high above. We watch it descend down to the woodland floor where it alights on a blade of grass, nodding it ever so slightly. It has a curious movement, arching its whole body to achieve forwards motion and waving to and fro in search of new purchase. Again, I have no idea what moth or butterfly the caterpillar will become at some point.

We make our way up the western face of the Knott, off the path. At the top, our movement through the bracken disturbs moths who take flight all around us. Once we get close enough to a settled individual, we can see that the moth is small and has brown wings with distinctive lines of darker and lighter tones running horizontally from wing tip to wing tip. I think (after consulting the field guide) that it is a brown silver line moth, at home in the wood and active in May to June. The brown silver line moth's caterpillars feed on the plentiful bracken. We leave them to settle, where they can rest in preparation for their night-time wanderings.

We descend the southern slope and begin climbing again up to the Great Beech. The bees are still busy around the scar on the trunk, and we decide that they must be fully settled. We watch them for a while, although Jim is not so keen.

We continue on, heading east along the southern edge, through the firs and then the stand of beech, all now in green leaf. Before too long we reach the five-bar gate. I want to check on the lords and ladies beside the main track and on the way to the arch and so we head in that direction. There is noticeable new growth beginning to crowd the path.

Before long, I spot the large arrow-shaped leaves, but there is still no flower. Upon closer inspection, I discover that the flower never had a chance to develop; something, presumably a deer, has bitten nearly the whole flower down to its base, in amongst the leaves. A little further on, and by way of compensation, the sweet woodruff described to you in an earlier entry is now in full flower. The four white petals of each flower form a cross about half a centimetre wide and are in clusters all over the patch of plant. The sweet woodruff is known for its sweet scent, and I am pleased to see it in flower.

A fitting end for today's visit.

TWENTY-FOUR

OF THE HORSE CHESTNUT

Sunday, 26 May 2019 – 07.10

There is something of an international feel to the entry today. For a start, I am cheating a little because I am writing the draft of this entry up on the 3 June 2019, a few days after this particular trip, and I am doing so sat on the balcony of our little apartment overlooking the bay of Saint George in the quiet seaside village of Agios Georgios. All while the crystal clear Ionian Sea laps very gently on the shore of the sandy beach a short distance away and while the swallows dance in the air and dart in and out of their neat little mud cup nest, perched on the wooden beam nestled in the eaves above my head.

I am not really cheating; I have my notes and my photos with me.

The second reason is that on the 26th I was accompanied by my Czech friend. It was his first trip to the wood, and I was excited to show him the wonders of the English countryside. He was impressed by the size of the wood and the diversity of the tree and plant species. He told me something of the conifers, beech, birch and rowan that make up the woods of his home in the mountains in the Czech Republic. I would like to visit his woods sometime, but I am comforted by the knowledge that we will not be stumbling across wolf, boar or bear on the trip today.

It is a very pleasant and warm late spring morning. We take my new favourite and now familiar walk through Brookside Lane, past the lords and ladies – the flower now turning to seed – and past the ramsons on the bank of the brook, also now starting to go over. When we reach the upper pasture, the green woodland canopy, illuminated in sunshine, stretches to the horizon. There are greens of many shades and hues, and I am proud.

Just before we enter the wood, I spot a new flower, at least for me, nestled in amongst the ever-growing grass a little outside the wood edge (I don't have my field guide in Corfu, so I will settle for a description for now, and then I will identify the plant when I get home). The yellow-flowered plant has leaves in opposing pairs up the stem, and the leaves are around four to five centimetres in length and their shape is long and thin and heavily sawtoothed around the edges but with rounded nodes. The leaves have a feather-like appearance. The plant stands around twenty to thirty centimetres tall and the stems are smooth. The distinctive yellow flowers, again arranged in opposing pairs towards the top of the plant, grow out horizontally from green pods and comprise an arched hood covering the stamens, with a smaller petal below.

When we enter the cool northern edge, I notice immediately

that the spring flowers are just starting to go over. I am glad that I have taken the time to describe them when I was able to, but I am a little saddened.

I want one final check on the rhododendron today to see if it is still in full flower and to see if the common figwort mentioned in the last entry is also in flower. So, we head in that direction. I will try and mix it up a bit from here on in.

On our way, my Czech friend spots something I have not noticed before; there are two trees growing side by side – a sycamore and an oak – both semi-mature. There is nothing in itself unusual in that; both species are plentiful in the wood. But what is unusual is that at the bases of the two trees, they appear to be conjoined in a bridge – or perhaps better described as a saddle – the smooth bark of the sycamore melding into the more fissured scaly bark of the oak. And where they meet, the two barks are rippled, where the growth of one pushes against the growth of the other, but give the appearance of one tree – as one, but yet not the same.

We continue on, along the winding path, between the maturing bracken and between oak and sycamore. I spot a holly in flower; rather scruffy and unspectacular. The white cluster of four-petalled flowers and yellow stamens are located at the base of the glossy, prickly leaves, where they meet the dark wood of the stems. The flowers are not nearly as nice as when they give way to the festive red berries.

We enter the glade and into full sunshine. I am surprised by how much the bracken stems have grown in only a week. On the edge of the glade, the rhododendron is pretty in pink. The balls of flowers coat every surface and form a beautiful picture against the surrounding green backdrop. Another week and their lustre will be gone. I have not been in the right place and at the right time to see the rhododendron in full flower for a long time, probably not since Dad was still able to come up the wood, and I am reminded of him now.

Before we leave the glade, I spot a juvenile oak, only just above head height but with a strong and healthy crown. On one particular branch, surrounded by the perfect oak leaves, there is a cluster of curious wooden balls. I have been on the lookout for examples of these to describe to you for a while. I have always been fascinated by them, ever since Dad first pointed them out to me as a small boy.

The balls are perfectly spherical, almost as if man had a hand in their turning. The balls are smooth and woody and about two centimetres across. I know them as oak apples, but they are of course not apples at all, and actually, I think these examples are oak marble galls. Oak apples have a paler, less woody appearance but are spherical and around the same size. If you were to cut one of our oak marble galls in half, you might find a pale-coloured grub in a chamber in the middle; it is the larvae of a gall wasp. The examples we find today are last year's I think, because each perfect round ball has a perfect single exit hole.

In undertaking some research, it is apparent that there are many different types of galls and therefore gall wasps. Some galls form on the leaves (above and below), some form on acorns and they come in many different shapes, sizes and colours and are not just limited to appearing on oaks.

The galls on my little oak belong, I think, to the gall wasp with the name of *Andricus kollari*. The gall is produced from a chemical released by the hatching larvae which triggers a reaction in the oak to grow the gall and in doing so creates a home and ready-made package of food for the larvae until it is ready to emerge as a fully formed tiny gall wasp, whereupon the cycle will be repeated.

Incidentally, on an earlier trip, I noticed that the solitary oak on the top of Knobbly Knott has a leaf that has a hard and green waxy type irregular lump on its top side; I wonder if that too is not the result of another type of gall wasp – I will have another look on my next visit.

I have known for some time that the gall, or oak apple, was prized prior to the invention of modern inks; presumably, the galls were crushed and mixed with water or a 'fixer' to produce ink for writing.

As you would expect, given their appearance, there is folklore associated with the oak apple. If you were to open an oak apple on Michaelmas Day (29 September) and find a worm, then you can expect the remainder of the year to be without incident. If, however you were to find a spider, then beware, for then you are in for a bad year!

We have an Oak Apple Day falling on 29 May, celebrating the return of King Charles II in 1660 and relating to his escape and place of hiding within an oak tree.

All that from the fascinating little woody balls.

I want to show my Czech friend Knobbly Knott and so we continue on, traversing eastwards the slope that rises steadily to the southern edge. On our way, I look out for the common figwort to see if it is yet in flower, but either I am sufficiently distracted by our pleasant conversation, or the plant has gone, for I do not spot it – I will look harder next time.

The beeches on top of the Knott are now covered in the hard green and bristly beech mast.

Whilst at the top, and in discussing tree species – including comparing names of the sweet chestnut in English and Czech – I spot a solitary horse chestnut in full flower. I am sure that this is the only specimen within the bounds of the wood itself. So, I think it appropriate that we learn something of the horse chestnut now.

The horse chestnut is a large tree with a domed canopy. It is deciduous; that is to say that it loses its leaves in the autumn. New buds form soon after and are sticky to the touch. The bark has a grey-brown colour and is scaly. The example in the wood has white flowers covering the canopy which are conical in shape. The leaves are large and comprise up to seven leaflets with the central leaflet being the largest and overall, up to twenty-five centimetres long. The fruit of the horse chestnut is the conker; they grow within the conker shell which is green and spiky and around four to five centimetres across. The conker, which is a red-brown colour with a shiny skin and pale scar, grows to between three and four centimetres across.

Most people of my generation will remember the horse chestnut for one thing, and that is the game of conkers; each autumn, towards the end of September or beginning of October, Dad would take us to our favourite conkering spot, near the hall, where we would pick the dropped conkers from the ground by the side of the lane and pick any from the tree within easy reach. And when pickings within reach were meagre, or tantalising larger specimens could be seen higher up in the autumn canopy, a handy fallen branch would be used to throw up into the tree in an attempt to dislodge the green and spiky packaged conkers. Several attempts with throwing the log were often required before hitting the spot.

Armed with a few good-sized conkers, you would then return home to thread the conkers (usually with an old shoelace) ready for school on the Monday. Some friends had secret methods for hardening their prized conker, including soaking in vinegar and then baking in the oven. Once threaded and prepared, it was time for the game of conkers; this involved taking it in turns to hit your opponent's conker with your own, and whoever successfully smashed the other was the winner. A conker with successive wins would be a two'er, three'er and so on. By the end of the school week, the playground, or in our case the 'street' was littered with failed and broken conkers, alongside tattered hopes and prayers.

I wonder if the children of today still play conkers?

No trip up the wood with a new visitor would be complete without a glimpse of the Dower House. So, we make our way to the southern edge by the Great Beech – the bees are still present and at home. Leaning on the top rail of the fence at the wood edge, we can see beyond the scattering of sheep and fattening lambs and past the thistles and numerous ancient paddock ant mounds, the hulk of the ruin rising remote in the park.

We continue our journey but stop one final time to sample Jack-by-the-hedge (garlic mustard). We both agree that it has a subtle garlic flavour, but I alone detect a definite final note of mustard – hence the name.

Our journey through the Spring Wood is at an end.

It is time for us to venture into the Summer Wood of warm, and sometimes hot, sunshine, of continued growth and industry and choked dusty paths below the drone of a million tiny wings.

Postscript:

The yellow flower mentioned at the very beginning of the above entry is, I think, yellow rattle (*Rhinanthus minor*). Yellow rattle, which is at home in the meadow, grows to between twenty and forty centimetres in height and flowers from May to August.

PART THREE
SUMMER WOOD

TWENTY-FIVE

OF THE FOXGLOVE

Monday, 10 June 2019 – 15.00

We are back from our holiday in Corfu, and the Summer Wood is calling, despite the weather.

I head in via the main track. It has been a little while since I last used this route – the growth of the plants and grasses on the verge either side of the track is startling, giving the track a crowded summery feel. The unbroken cloud overhead is steely grey, and it is raining.

On my way to the arch, I pass bright red poppies in the long grasses and a weedy, straggling-looking plant with tiny yellow flowers. The plant is spindly and apologetic-looking and appearing like it would be more at home on a patch of urban wasteland rather than standing on the edge of the wild. It is growing to around forty to fifty centimetres high with segmented stem and leaves that are lance shaped with pointy lobes. The leaves at the base of the plant have a different appearance, being multi-lobed – a bit like a small sycamore leaf. The flowers are bright yellow and are formed in clusters at the end of the stems. Each flower, comprising four cross-shaped petals, is no more than half a centimetre across. According to my field guide, the plant is hedge mustard (*Sisymbrium officinale*). It is a perennial plant which flowers from April to November and is at home on wasteland and in the hedgerows. Other names for hedge mustard include 'wiry Jack' and 'singer's plant'. In folklore, it was believed that hedge mustard was a cure for sore throats, hence the name 'singer's plant'.

A little further on along the track I pass a dog rose (*Rosa canina*) in flower. Dog rose is a shrub, with thorny, reddy green stems. The leaves branch off the main stems and are arranged in opposing pairs of around six leaflets and terminate in a single central leaflet. The five petals of the flowers are pink, fading to white towards the yellow middle, and around five centimetres across.

Growing close to the dog rose is a plant which I know to be a dead nettle or white dead nettle (*Lamium album*). It looks just like the stinging nettle but is completely harmless. The leaves, staggered along the hairy square stem, are oval shaped and heavily sawtoothed, descending in size towards the top of the plant. The flowers are evenly distributed up the stem above where the leaves adjoin. The flowers comprise a hooded single petal covering the stamens and lower petal, all white in colour.

I pass to the side of the arch and into the wet wood. Leaves and trunks glisten in the wet all-round, but the path is still firm underfoot. I turn immediately right, heading west, just inside of the northern edge. The wood is noticeably green, having lost the array of varied colour from the spangled display of spring flowers. And the canopy cover overhead is nearly complete, creating a gloom within the wood, accentuated by the heavy cloud. But my spirits are high; there is no bad time to be up the wood.

Along with the bracken, the bramble is growing fast, with new green shoots reaching out in determined exploration over the ever-narrowing path. And all-round, the bramble is in white flower with promise of fruits to come in a few weeks' time.

Instead of taking my usual route to cross the converging streams, I continue on along the southern edge and eventually find myself in a very wet area enfolded by the surrounding foliage. Growing out from the marshy wet ground are tall plants comprising narrow stems at the base, branching out into vertical tall leaves to nearly chest height. I think the plant is white flag, yellow flag or maybe even reed mace. I will be visiting this spot again to check on their progress.

I am drawn back to the rhododendron glade, not consciously but more just by following my nose. The bracken continues to march on and in some places is already head height. Within the glade, beside the path edge, is probably my most favourite flower, and that is the foxglove (*Digitalis*). I think my attraction to the foxglove stems from family holidays long ago up in the Lake District, where I have my first memories of them growing by stone walls and on the lower slopes of towering fells.

The specimens up the wood, and the one before me now, nodding ever so gently from the industrious actions of a rounded bumble bee, stands around chest height. The flowers, pink on this specimen, grow up a long, robust stem that emerges from a rosette of green-grey hairy leaves at the base. The flowers are trumpet shaped with deeper purple-white ringed spots on the inside. From observation, I know that the rosette forms in the first year, steadily growing in size, before the stems and flowers emerge in year two – making the plant biennial.

I may have mentioned before, but a few years ago, I came across what must have been hundreds of foxgloves of all different shades of pink growing in a large clearing of felled trees in the north-eastern part of the wood. I have visited the clearing at around this time of year many times since, but the display has not been repeated. The foxglove relies on seed distribution for continuity, with each flower producing seed pods containing many thousands of tiny black seeds.

The Old English name for foxglove is *foxes golfa*, and folklore suggests that the foxes donned the flowers on their paws to improve their cunning on the hunt. Of all the flowers in the wood, the foxglove is the most striking, most beautiful and unforgettable. Our garden in Wrights Bush, New Zealand was filled with foxgloves as a reminder of home.

I pass through the glade, allowing my hands to wander whimsically over the rough tops of the hastening bracken. I notice a relatively new burrow on the far edge of the glade, just off the path. Newly excavated soil is mounded up at the entrance and long scratch marks made by the claws of the industrious doe are visible in the moist soil.

A little further on, and in the partial shade of a juvenile sweet chestnut and in-between the bracken stems, I spot what must be the last bluebell flower, fresh and vibrant, in a world of green. All the more beautiful in its isolation. I continue on in the direction of the west face of Knobbly Knott and on the lookout for the common figwort, missed during the last trip.

I pass a solitary elder in flower, its clustered white flowers weighed down heavy by the rain. It is not long, with full attention this time, before I spot the figwort, and I have to say, I am a little underwhelmed. For such a big plant, the flowers, out of proportion with its impressive height and the size of the leaves, are tiny. They are curious though, comprising a larger couple of petals forming a hood above the opening, revealing the stamens and three further petals below. The upper petals are deep purple in colour at the tips, fading to yellow. Common figwort (*Scrophularia nodosa*) is a perennial plant flowering from June to July. Other names for the plant include 'heal all', 'throatwort' and 'pilewort'. Folklore has it that the plant was used as a cure for piles. And the name 'figwort' is derived from the Latin *ficus* meaning 'fig' as piles supposedly have the appearance of a fig.

When I arrive at the base of Knobbly Knott, and after turning north, I come across a tree nursery in amongst the long grasses, where a number of juvenile oaks and sweet chestnuts compete for space and light with the surrounding brambles. They are the next generation of trees waiting patiently for the inevitable fate of their mature parents towering overhead.

I make my way up the western face, off the path and past a one-time coppiced mature sweet chestnut. At the top, I take the opportunity to check on the waxy green lumps on the upside of the leaves on the solitary oak. I remain convinced that the slightly alien-looking growths are the actions of a gall wasp and will continue to observe over the coming weeks.

I head off the top, down the southern edge and past sycamores already going to seed and up to the Great Beech, where I turn right, skirting the southern edge, heading west. Lost in thought, and hunkered down in my coat against the persistent rain, I pass a large patch of foxglove rosettes to the side of the path – they will be a picture this time next year. A little further on, I spot a large plant I do not recognise. It stands around sixty centimetres high and you have the impression that it is not done growing yet. The leaves are large – nearly twenty-five centimetres long and a similar dimension in width, with distinctive veins, ovate in shape and with a wavy edge. Despite in-depth consultation of my field guide and other sources, I have no clue of the name; we shall have to wait to see if it flowers.

I continue on along the path that traverses the southern slope, snipping the odd encroaching bramble leader as I go and past the northern sett, its occupants safe and sound away from the light of the day.

Before long, I arrive at the shrine. Offerings continue to be made to the gods of the wood and the sprites and the dryads and not forgetting the fairy folk. And while I may call it the shrine, some small hand has kindly clarified this curiosity through a neat little wooden sign suspended from a twig above the cluttered altar top. The sign confidently announces: 'Fairy Meeting Place'. As if I did not know.

The rain continues to fall steadily.

My thoughts and the general peace of the wood are abruptly broken by the wrenching, tearing and cracking of timber a short way off to my right, as a tired old limb in full leaf succumbs to the weight of the rain and weakened joints. Its passage down to the ground is short but energetic, ending in a resounding 'thump'. On closer inspection, it is a sycamore branch and not insubstantial – I would not like to have been underneath it! Just as the wood itself is a living organism, each species in general harmony, the surfaces of the fallen branch are covered in lichens of different forms and shades of green and yellow – some stalked, others in long yellow matts and lobed varieties, rather alien and unwholesome in appearance. It is clear that I could have an entire chapter on lichens – we shall see.

I am heading back in generally the same direction I have

come from so branch off at random, following a lesser path and my nose. Very quickly, it is apparent that I am on a path I have not used before, or at least not that I can recall, because I am in unfamiliar surroundings, with landform and vistas entirely and obviously new to me. I had thought and taken for granted that I knew the wood and all its ways well, but it appears that there are still surprises. For a while, I am disorientated but not alarmingly so. I had thought that the route would take me north-west, skirting Knobbly Knott, but after five or so minutes I find myself back in familiar surroundings, just south of the Knott and on the path up to the Great Beech. I turn left, up to the Knott (again) and turn east just to the side of the summit, before turning north and taking the long slope down into the valley, past what I think of as recently planted trees (following the clear felling of a large area of the old wood), but which is, in actual fact, probably now around twenty years of growth.

Just before reaching the shallow valley bottom, I pass a patch of black dishevelled feathers fanned out on the leaf litter. They belong, I think, to an unfortunate blackbird.

I am close to the arch now, but before I reach it, I stop awhile to listen to a thrush, high up in a gnarly old oak, singing for all she is worth.

TWENTY-SIX

OF MIDSUMMER

Friday, 21 June 2019 – sunset

It is midsummer – the summer solstice and the longest day. Where, from here on in, imperceptibly, the daylight hours will grow shorter, and we will creep ever so slowly towards autumn and the end of our story.

I am up the wood at last light.

Over my right shoulder, the sun sets behind the hills in the distance, lighting up the scattered cloud in brilliant oranges and reds. I pass large black slugs on the path – I think they are simply called 'large black slugs'. I leave them to their slow-motion wanderings. Just before I pass to the side of the arch, I spot the mesmerising flash of white from the tail of a rabbit on the path a hundred or so yards in front.

The wood as usual is filled with birdsong, and I can hear the blackbird, thrush and robin, singing out territories and bidding farewell to the day. A tawny owl hoots far off in the distance. I have purpose this evening; I want to see if the northern sett is active and so head in that direction, via the crossroads on the main track and up and over Knobbly Knott.

By the time I arrive at the sett, it is end of the day and the birds have gone to roost, hidden out of the way and safe. I prop myself against the aged scaly trunk of a nearby tree, keeping downwind, and wait in silent anticipation. It is not long before a striped black and white head bobs up warily from the dark mass of the sett opening – it is nearly dark and shapes and forms in the low light are losing their definition. The badger emerges and is quickly gone, shambling up the slope away from me and into the undergrowth close to the wood edge. But I can hear the badger moving about, rustling and snuffling amongst the summer vegetation.

A short while later, and it is heading back down the slope but curiously going backwards and appearing to shuffle dried plant material with its forelegs, presumably to renew bedding within the sett. It disappears from view but only briefly, re-emerging and quickly back up the slope again and out of sight. A short time later, a second head appears from the same opening but more warily, bobbing in and out of view, and I wonder whether they know I am here, despite my stealth.

There is a subtle clicking sound out there in the dark. I cannot tell where from or what by, and I am left wondering if it is the badgers that are the source. The series of quickly repetitive clicks are only just audible, but they are there – it is not my imagination.

I watch the badgers for a few more minutes until they are nearly lost to the dark and then move off quietly, not wishing to disturb them. I make my way along the southern and western edge in nearly full dark, disturbing what must be a deer somewhere nearby – it takes flight, moving deeper into the wood.

As I reach the northern edge, I can hear the raucous jackdaws and crows making a racket from the roosts out in the parkland to the south – something must be bothering them. I leave the wood via the arch and main track into the near dark on this, the longest, day – it is ten-forty.

When I arrive at my car, I look back; the wood is a dark mass on the horizon below the blue-black sky. Directly above the centre line of the wood is a planet, a bright point of light in the dark, endless expanse.

TWENTY-SEVEN
OF THE UNEXPECTED

Saturday, 29 June 2019 – 14.00

It is hot, not stifling but nearly. The shade of the wood offers some respite.

The air within is humid and heavy with the heady earthy smell of the wood following the recent rains. Pockets of sunshine burst through the canopy, lighting the woodland floor here and there. The birds are quiet, apart from the ever-present gangs of tits foraging through the canopies on the hunt for a meal.

The wood is unusually quiet and free of other visitors for this time of day on a Saturday. I am not complaining.

I said early on that I would share some stories with you from my trips up the wood; I am reminded now of this particular story, due to the heat. It is a recent story from either last year or the year before, a very peculiar one and entirely unexpected, especially for the wood.

It was a hot day, much like today, and I was joined by my youngest. We were in the southern part of the wood, with the woodland edge and parkland beyond to our left, and moving through the young beeches. We were lost in idle conversation, or rather, Jim was probably sharing her latest cunning plan with me – as quickly forgotten as mentioned – when out of nowhere, well, actually from the path ahead, came the naked wood runner.

As fast as he was upon us, he was gone. His only attire were trainers and shin-high old man white socks. But that is all. All else of his rather aged and pasty wiry body was exposed to the woodland air. He had the audacity to say 'good morning' as he passed, and far too late, my reply was something like 'weirdo'.

And then we were left laughing and a little in shock.

On one level, I kind of get it, in terms of being at one with nature in the wood, where I am most at home, but I wonder whether he had other, less noble motives, given the day and the hour. If you happen to be reading this, it was not big and was not clever.

And where did he keep his clothes?

It was definitely a first for me and probably best left as a one-off experience.

TWENTY-EIGHT
OF THE SNAKE

Saturday, 6 July 2019 – 09.00

It is pleasantly warm this sunny morning and I am on the hunt. This time, it is for the snake.

Although early spring on a sunny day is a good time to spot an adder in England, the adder remains active throughout April/May to October. It prefers open country, such as heath and moor, but I know that they are up the wood.

A long time ago, Dad and I were making our way along the very southern edge, off the path at the top of the deer bank, when we unwittingly disturbed a basking adder coiled in the warm sunshine. We caught only a glimpse as it made its escape noisily and at surprising speed through the leaf litter. Being a young lad, I tried to follow, but bramble and general undergrowth meant continued pursuit was impossible.

So, I make my way along the main track, heading for the five-bar gate. When I arrive, with the open view of the sunshine-washed parkland before me, I check for dragonflies – it is a little too early and, as expected, there are none.

I carry on, turning right and eventually arrive at the Great Beech. Instead of heading down the track to the path at the base of the deer bank, I stick to the fence line – well, as much as the advancing bramble and bracken will allow – and proceed as quietly as possible.

Adders can detect vibrations through the woodland floor, so stealth is important.

But it is no good, and after twenty or so minutes of struggling through clinging understorey, I concede defeat and drop down into the wood and onto the open path. I knew I would have to be very lucky to spot an adder, but I am not deterred and will have another go when the conditions are right.

TWENTY-NINE

OF DAMSELS AND BUTTERFLIES

Sunday, 14 July 2019 – 15.30

This entry was meant to be about the sweet chestnut, but as usual the wood had other ideas. Jim Bob and I take the Brookside Lane route from the greens, walking in dappled sunlight and shade. I notice that the ramsons, which only a few weeks ago lit up the far bank of the brook, have almost completely died down. And the same can be said of those growing by the side of the path near to the burial ground. We emerge out of the shade of the narrow, sunken path into the grassy meadow, bathed in full sunshine.

I do not know why it necessarily surprises me, but I am shocked by the growth of the grasses and plants generally since the last time I walked in via this route. Our attention is soon distracted by the myriad butterflies and other insects in the air and in amongst the grasses all around.

Technically, this journal is about the wood, but I am too taken by the living meadow, and its diversity of life all around us, to not mention our discoveries on what can only be described as an invertebrate safari. Butterflies dance in the summer air, alighting on meadow flowers, only to quickly move onto the next, making photo opportunities rare. We watch as different species interact with each other in their aerial antics.

Our first butterfly, of which there are many, and, according to my field guide, is the gatekeeper, apparently common in the Midlands. The gatekeeper has a wingspan of around 3.7 to four centimetres, and when settled long enough to observe, wings folded, they have orange edges with the remainder in tans and browns. The most distinctive feature of this proliferate butterfly is a large black dot on each underside wing, on the orange background centred with two bright white pin pricks (presumably evolved to look just like a large eye to ward off predators). The caterpillars of the gatekeeper feed on the local grasses.

The next most common butterfly, at least today in this spot, is the marbled white and, according to the guide, is our only distinctively black and white chequered butterfly and is proving to be harder to photograph than the gatekeeper (I'm currently lying on the path while my willing assistant is out somewhere in the meadow chasing a number of specimens). The marbled white has a wingspan of four to 4.5 centimetres and is at home in the south and the Midlands – the guide says it can be found on chalk and limestone grassland, but it must be equally happy on ironstone grassland!

By far and away the prettiest and most striking insect this afternoon is not a butterfly but a day-flying moth. Its wings are 'V' shaped, swept back and jet black with bright red spots. Beautiful! It is the six-spot burnet and common on grassland across the country. This particular specimen is photographed settled on a cerise pink flower, which I will (hopefully) identify in a bit.

Flying in amongst the other butterflies are rather ragged-looking dark brown specimens. After much consideration, and given the very dark brown appearance, I have settled on them being the ringlet. The difficulty I have had is that the one example that stayed still long enough for Jim Bob to get a photograph was very ragged in appearance – I can only assume the ragged appearance is a result of battle scars or just old age. Anyway, the name ringlet must arise from the distinctive rings, or dots, on both the upside and underside of the wings. Only, the example we found was so ragged that the ringlets were absent. The ringlet is at home close to the shade of the woods and hedgerows and has a wingspan of around four centimetres.

Of all the butterflies on this sunny afternoon, the easiest to identify without having to get close to is the large white. Distinctive due to its size and the white colouring, and familiar to gardeners cross the land, the large white's favourite egg-laying place is on cabbages and cauliflowers, and the consequent caterpillars are unwelcome pests. The large white has a wingspan of around six centimetres.

The last of the butterflies, at least for today, is small, with orange-brown colouring and with a distinctive overlapping wing configuration. I think it is the small skipper and rather beautiful. I thought at first that it was another day-flying moth due to its chunkier, hairier body, but it is not. This small butterfly is again common in the Midlands and has a wingspan of 2.2–2.5 centimetres.

Accompanying the butterflies and the moth are one of my favourite aerial insects – the damselflies. There are two specimens flying around and about – the first has a blue and black colouring. Generally, each segment of the abdomen (the part behind the wings and legs) has blue sides with a black lengthways dash. After some research, I think it is the common blue damselfly. Identification is difficult because there are a few blue-black coloured damselflies present in the UK. The common blue flies between May and August and can be seen throughout the UK but is particularly common in the south and the Midlands. The second specimen is dull green-black in colour; again, after some research, I think it is the female of the common blue.

The last of the airborne insects to describe for you today, and the most noticeable, is the dragonfly. Significantly larger than the damselflies, we both watch the solitary specimen, 'hawking' backwards and forwards over the tops of the grasses and meadow flowers, scattering other insects in its wake. It is a little way off and moving fast, but it has green and blue colouring and I suspect it is the emperor dragonfly. According to the British Dragonfly Society, it is the bulkiest of the UK dragonflies and can be seen from June through to August.

And finally, for this entry, all-round us can be heard the crickets and the grasshoppers. They can be hard to spot, and harder still to identify, but if you are patient, and once you have your 'eye in', they can be found. We spot two different specimens today; the first is a reasonable size – around three centimetres in length with brown and green colouring. Of note, it has a distinctive creamy green crescent on its shoulder, setting it apart from other varieties. I think it is Roesel's bush cricket which can be found in long grass throughout the Midlands and the south-east.

The next specimen is almost entirely green but with darker green to black markings along its abdomen. It also has black eyes with a noticeable short black line behind each eye – according to the field guide, I think it is the common field grasshopper, growing to be between 1.2 to two centimetres in length and found throughout the UK.

This journey through the meadow is taking far longer than expected, but there are a couple of flowers that I must record.

The first is bright cerise pink, or perhaps purple in colour, growing at the end of thin stems around thirty to forty centimetres in height. The leaves are arranged alternately up the stem and are lance shaped with small serrations to the edges. The flowers are basically a ball of pink. According to my guide, the plant is common knapweed (*Centaurea nigra*) which flowers from June to September.

Beside the knapweed are small, white individual flowers which appear to have ten petals, but which are in fact five petals that are so deeply notched that they have the appearance of ten. And sitting on top of the white petals, there are a further five green petals alternately dividing the white petals. This flower is proving illusive to identify, but I will keep trying.

Deep down in the grasses is a delicate flower arranged in opposing pairs at the end of the stems, and in the example I am observing now, one flower is yellow, and the opposite flower is orangey red. The leaves are smaller than the flowers and trefoil in shape, not dissimilar to clover but 'pointier'. According to my *Collins Gem Guide*, I think the flower belongs to bird's-foot trefoil (*Lotus corniculatus*). Other names for the bird's-foot trefoil include 'Eggs and Bacon' (due to the colouring) and 'Tom Thumb'. The name 'bird's-foot' comes from the shape of the seed pods which, when formed, have an appearance a lot like a bird's clawed foot. The plant is common in grassland and flowers from May through to September.

I cannot properly convey to you just how alive the meadow and this moment in time and space is, from the crickets beyond count in the grasses and meadow flowers, to the butterflies, damselflies and solitary dragonfly crisscrossing in flight everywhere you look, to the swifts and house martens above our heads – a very good example of habitat that can be created if nature is just left to her own devices.

It has taken us a little over half an hour to move through the meadow, compared to the five or so minutes it would normally take us, and now we arrive in the shade of the northern edge. The wood and its equal wonders beckon.

Once in, we turn immediately right (noting the green fruits on the hazel at the entrance); I want to check on the plants growing in the very marshy spot I came across a few weeks ago.

On the way, there are large swathes of plants growing at the path edge, standing between shin and knee height – another one I have been keeping my eye on and now they are in flower. The stems are hairy, and the leaves are large, oval in shape and deeply veined. The flowers are white and arranged up the stem. The petals are small and folded in, forming a pocket/purse enclosing the noticeably protruding stamens. I think it is enchanter's nightshade (*Circaea lutetiana*). A perennial which flowers from June to August and is happy in the deep shade of the wood.

We arrive at the marshy spot, but the tall plants with their feet in standing pools of still water show no signs of flowering. We continue on, over the converging streams and up the western edge, heading north. The squirrels are very active on the woodland floor, and we must disturb upwards of fifteen to twenty of them on our way. We continue on in the direction of the Knott, passing through the rhododendron glade and through the head height, dense bracken.

The final new plant we spot today has purple flowers;

at first glance I thought it was bugle, but it is not. The plant stands about fifteen to twenty centimetres high, with opposing oval– to lance-shaped darker green leaves. The hooded purple flowers emerge out of a flower head that looks a little like the construction of a fir cone. According to my field guide, the plant is called self-heal (*Prunella vulgaris*), which is a perennial, flowering from June to September and at home in the wood. Other names for the plant include: 'healwort', 'woundwort' and 'sicklewort'. The name of the plant, as it suggests, stems from a long association with its general healing properties.

At the western base of the Knott, and in deciding which way to go, we stop awhile to watch hoverflies and other woodland insects flying in an aerial ballet within a bright and hazy shaft of sunlight piercing through the canopy above. Jim Bob decides that they are not insects at all but rather fairy folk enjoying the warm summer sun. I think we may have all thought this from time to time.

At about the same time as I am showing Jim Bob the tree nursery I spotted a couple of entries ago, we receive a call from home reminding us about dinner time. Our time enjoying the meadow means we have to cut the trip short. And I am reminded to turn off my phone when I am away from civilisation!

So, we hurry on, and after twenty or so minutes we are back out in the meadow, still bathed in sunshine.

A lark, ascending overhead, sings its solitary unbroken song as we head home.

For singing till his heaven fills,
'T is love of earth that he instils,
And ever winging up and up,

Our valley is his golden cup,
And he the wine which overflows

The Lark Ascending (excerpt)
George Meredith

Postscript:

The wild raspberries mentioned in chapter 3 are now fruiting and should be ready for picking soon.

In consultation with my ecologist colleague, we have settled on lesser stitchwort (*Stellaria graminea*) for the white flowers in this chapter.

THIRTY

OF DOCK AND NETTLE

Sunday, 21 July 2019 – 14.00

I decide upon the Brookside Lane route again this afternoon, simply because of how much I enjoyed the walk through the meadow and its world of wonder last week. On my way, I spot a dragonfly trawling back and forth with purpose over the tops of the nodding grasses, before I reach the open expanse of the top meadow. The winged primeval insect is too quick to properly identify and does not settle. But, as it passes close to me overhead, I can see that its distended body is a rusty red colour and is a good size – perhaps as much as eight centimetres long, with yellowy coloured filigree wings expertly slicing the air. After some research, I think this specimen, ancestor of colossal monsters, could be a brown hawker. The brown hawker flies between June and September.

It is overcast and perhaps the meadow is a little quieter, but

I still spot the odd butterfly, and the crickets, of which there must be thousands, must be chirruping all around me. I spot a new butterfly to add to those spotted last week – according to the field guide, I think it is the meadow brown – it is less colourful than the gatekeeper, darker brown in colour with orange tips to the main wings with a distinctive black dot centred with a single white pin prick. The meadow brown is very common and flies from June to mid-August.

I also spot a couple more meadow flowers to mention. The first I already know is yarrow (*Achillea millefolium*) and present in my own lawn at home. The plant stands around thirty centimetres tall and has feathery type leaves arranged up the bending stem. The white flowers grow in clusters around six centimetres across at the end of the stems, but each four-petalled flower is maybe half a centimetre across. Other names for yarrow include: 'woundwort', 'devil's plaything' and, curiously, 'nosebleed'. Folklore has it that yarrow, picked at night under a full moon and placed under a pillow, would bring on dreams of a future lover.

A little further, and in amongst bird's-foot trefoil and grasses, there are large patches of golden yellow, belonging, I think, to lady's bedstraw (*Galium verum*). The tiny yellow-green flowers grow in abundant clusters at the top of the stems. The leaves are spaced out in whorls up the stem and again have a delicate, feathery appearance. Lady's bedstraw flowers between June and September and common names include 'cheese rennet', 'wild rosemary' and 'maiden's hair'. The cheese rennet name stems from the use of the plant for the curdling and colouring of milk in cheesemaking.

As I enter the wood, the path is framed by two common plants that I have been meaning to mention for a while. Not because they are in any way spectacular but because, at least for my generation, they were probably the first wild plants that you were familiar with at an early age – I am referring of course to the humble dock and the nettle. And the reason that we are familiar with them is the sting of the nettle for the unaware and the relief that can be offered by the sap of the dock.

You knew very quickly from a young age that if you were unlucky enough to get stung by a nettle (as I was frequently), the worst of it could be abated by rubbing a dock leaf vigorously between your hands and applying the soggy green concoction to the fast-reddening area. I do not know, and perhaps some research will reveal more, whether it is the make-up of the dock sap or just the cooling effect (from evaporation) or a combination of the two that provides relief, but whatever, I think it works.

The nettle, or common nettle (*Urtica dioica*), is recognisable from its angled square stems and serrated hairy leaves that are oval in shape, arranged in opposing pairs and which descend in size towards the top of the plant. The example before me now, part of a rather scruffy patch of nettle plants, stands about adult waste height. It is at this time of year that the nettle produces its flowers. The flowers are green to red-brown in colour and hang in a rather untidy string-type fashion from the stem, protruding from the base of the leaves.

The nettle is more useful and versatile than you think. It is a home and source of food for a number of different minibeasts and by reason of this, has an important part to play in ecology and biodiversity. From the human perspective, and I know because I have experimented, the younger leaves, when boiled, make a good spinach substitute, and they can also be used fresh or dried to make nettle tea, a good source of vitamins. The boiling of the leaves removes the hairy texture and importantly the sting. And if you fancy a snack on the run, quickly pinch the tender very top leaves of the plant, 'grasp the nettle' as it were, and vigorously rub the nettle between your palm to disarm the stings, then the leaves are quite edible and palatable.

In addition to a food source, the stems of the nettle can be dried to make cordage. Again, I have tried this– you crush the stems flat, and they then separate along the segmentation and into lengths of cord. The cord can then be braided/spliced to create longer lengths.

I have heard, although I cannot remember where, that there is some evidence that nettles, either through ingestion or through intentional stinging, reduces the symptoms of hay fever. I think I may try the intentional stinging next year, but I am not suggesting in any way that you try it! In folklore, a bunch of nettle tops thrown onto a fire during a storm would protect your home from lightning strikes.

The humble dock does not get mention in my field guides. Its proper name, at least the variety I am observing now, growing cheek by jowl with the nettle, is curly dock (*Rumex crispus*). The dock has an overall untidy appearance. The oval leaves of the curly dock are more lance shaped than those of the broad-leaved dock and have a wavy edge. The flowers comprise a single round green petal with paler green centre. The plant is around fifty to sixty centimetres high.

On entering the wood, I turn immediately right, heading west. The cloud overhead and dense canopy combine to create a mid-afternoon gloom. The wood is silent, save for the backdrop of leaves stirring very gently in the canopy tops and low drone of a million tiny wings. There is an intimacy to the wood at such times, where there is perpetual shade and views out from the path are closely confined by the dense summer foliage.

I catch a hint of movement to my right and, upon careful

investigation, spot a tiny wren, bobbing curiously on the spot with his upright speckled tail and calling to its mate (or possibly fledged chick) nearby but out of sight. The wren is one of our smallest birds and easily identified by its often bolt upright short tale. I think I have said before that it is my favourite bird, and I cannot help feeling there is an air of mysticism about it, perhaps by reason of its secretive nature. Folklore tells us of the old custom of the 'Hunting of the Wren', where on 26 December – St Stephen's Day – a captured and impaled wren would be paraded aloft through the streets to music by the Wren Boys or Mummers.

In the now much mentioned marshy spot, the tall upright plants remain stubbornly without flower. I will keep trying but leave mention until such a time, as I have more to report.

I arrive at the painter's crossroads with the Knott ascending in front of me. I suppose it is time now that I share my story about the painter. It was around the same time of year, a couple of years ago, that Ollie and I were on an afternoon walk on a warm summer's afternoon, making our way down off the Knott, when we stumbled upon the painter and his apprentice, easels set up and going about their craft, brush and palette in hand. They would probably have preferred to have been left alone – I suspect I would – but curiosity got the better of me and so I stopped and introduced myself.

It is impossible to convey in words just how perfect the painter's well-progressed work was – a moment in time in the wood cast by skilled hand on the canvas; every green blade of grass, woodland plant, grey trunk, twisting branch, twig and leaf captured for all eternity. The incomplete painting was photograph perfect in every minute detail, but it was more than that; it captured the very essence of the vibrancy and vitality of the wood. I can see the painting now as I am writing this.

We spoke of the wood and its wonders, all while I did my best to deter Ollie from showing too much interest in the painter's bag which clearly contained more than just artist's paraphernalia. The painter was quick to tell me something of the magic of the wood, of bright white lights spied between trunks and how he had been warned off being abroad within the wood after sundown. I told him of my own curious tale which I will tell you at the appropriate time. The conversation was brief, and I do not remember the painter's name, but I will never forget that painting. And I knew that from that point on, this spot, this junction of pathways deep within the wood, would forever be known as 'the painter's crossroads'.

I ignore the calling of the Knott for the time being and instead I turn left, heading east and shortly afterwards branch right, off the path. I am collecting photographs for a future chapter that will be entirely dedicated to fungi, but enough of that for now. I do inevitably, and as if by some unknown force, probably best known as habit, arrive on the top of the Knott below a brightening sky. I check on the leaves of the oak but can find no sign of the waxy growths previously mentioned. Around the base of the south side of the oak, lay scattered the remnants of last year's enormous fungi growth from a long way up the trunk, hinting at trouble within.

I sit on one of the many handy stumps at the top, just enjoying the warmth of the sun breaking through the thinning cloud. I watch the industrious activity of the larger-than-average ants (but not as big as proper wood ants) around my feet. I will not attempt to identify them, content instead to watch as they cart away the carcass of a small fly.

I continue my foray off path, down through the dense bracken covering the south-western slope, wondering whether I should get the missus to check me for ticks when I return home. Away from the southern toe, I stop again and settle on a fallen log, hoping for a glimpse maybe of deer. But instead, I watch large white butterflies and brown butterflies (perhaps ringlets) fly erratically in-between the trees a little way ahead.

Someone has carefully placed a spray of flowers at the base of the sister to the Great Beech, only a short distance from where we scattered a little of Dad's ashes. I wonder at the significance of the flowers and their story. I forget sometimes that the wood is someone else's special place too.

I turn right and have another go at tracking down a snake along the top of the deer bank but rather foolishly, given the time of day, and consequently, without surprise, with no luck. I am going to have to pick an early sunny and warm morning soon, before autumn is upon us.

It is not long before I drop down to the path and continue on, passing through bracken-choked, but otherwise sunny, glades. There are more butterflies to see, and I have a new one to describe for you; it looks a lot like the ringlet, nearly as brown and with the same ring dots. But this specimen has white speckles as well. I think it is the speckled wood butterfly. According to my field guide, the speckled wood is common in the south-east but more localised in the Midlands. As the name suggests, it too is a haunter of the wood. The speckled wood has a wingspan of around four centimetres and flies in two broods from April to early June and again from July to early September – clearly the second brood then.

Before the western edge, I head north-east and into the heart of the wood. Still on the lookout for new flowers (I think we are in the endgame now), I come across a single specimen, growing alone and in the shade on the woodland floor and definitely one I have not seen before. The plant stands around fifty centimetres high with a single stem. Broad, oval-shaped leaves grow from the base of the stem and thereafter descend noticeably in size spirally to the tip. The flowers have two distinct parts; five green petals are arranged in a winged star shape, followed by a central greeny, purply white flower asymmetrical in form. The flowers have a definite exotic appearance. After consulting the guide, I think it is broad-leaved helleborine (*Epipactis helleborine*). The plant is a member of the orchid family, and I am rather excited to have found an orchid growing in the midst of the wood. According to the guide, broad-leaved helleborine flowers July to August and is most at home in full shade below the dense canopies.

Back out in the meadow, and in full sun now, I spot a beautifully coloured smaller butterfly alighted on the shorter grass on the path in front of me. The wings are brightly coloured in oranges, blacks, yellows, whites and blues. I think it is the small tortoiseshell which has a wingspan of five centimetres.

Instead of exiting via the lane through the ornate kissing gate, I stick to the path through the meadows. On my way, I spot the final dragonfly of the day, but it does not stay still long enough for me to get a good look.

Back at the car, the thermometer reads twenty-three degrees. A precursor of the heat forecast for the next few days.

THIRTY-ONE
LORD OF THE FLIES

Thursday, 25 July 2019 – 19.15

It is hot. Very hot. I think the temperature peaked at thirty-six degrees late afternoon. It is the sort of heat which takes your breath away and which is normally reserved for that moment where you exit the air-conditioned plane on a far-flung summer holiday.

Anyway, I decide upon the Knightley Way path this evening, the start of which is up by the church. I park up in the lane with the warm-coloured stone church to my right. I am welcomed on the path by the unimpressive and unthreatening bark of a small dog glimpsed through the picket gate of the cottage to my left.

The last time I used this route, the path was frozen and dusted with snow. At the valley bottom, just past the young Nene, I pass under the weeping branches of a crab apple, its boughs weighed down by the fruit. I stoop low. The path is crowded with summer growth and below the arched canopies, the air is close and humid.

A little further on and growing on the steep bank of the sunken path is a plant with bright purple and yellow flowers. It straggles to around sixty to seventy centimetres high and appears to be clambering up and over the plants around it. The leaves are oval in shape and vary in size. The five purple petals of the flower are folded back, accentuating the bright yellow cone surrounding the stamens. The plant reminds me of deadly nightshade, but it is actually bittersweet (*Solanum dulcamara*). Bittersweet is a vine and flowers between May and September. As with deadly nightshade, the entire plant is poisonous. At first sight, it does have an unwholesome appearance. Another name for bittersweet is 'felonwort'.

I continue on, through the green, canopied tunnel and eventually through the kissing gate and up into the pasture. Instead of turning right, and for the first ever time, I head left, following a clear, well-walked path in the close-cropped grass. I am a little saddened to see that our wild flower meadow, beyond the hedge and on the rising ground to the left in the distance, is freshly cut and the hay arranged in tidy windrows ready for bailing. Cutting at this time of year is important for the health of the meadow, but I am nevertheless glad that I got to see it when I did.

On the opposite side of the pasture, I reach the wood edge, a wall of green beyond which the wood awaits in shade and shadow. There is a wooden bridge here (spied very early on in this journal) over a very dry ditch. Upon the wooden planks lay scattered halved hazelnut shells, evidence of hungry grey squirrels.

In the interior, the air is oppressive and heavy, and all is still with the weight of the heat. I follow the path to my right and before very long, I have attracted a small swarm of irritating flies buzzing around my head in the heat, desperate, I guess, for salt and moisture. They remain my constant companions.

I notice a curious low rushing, or whooshing noise, with each step; it is not an impending heart attack but the beating of a thousand tiny wings. Each time I pass understorey plants, including the bracken, hundreds of harmless hoverflies take flight, and for a brief moment it is these curious little insects that create the strange noise, literally with every other step. I can only conclude that these are the same insects that create the constant drone in the canopies above during the day but which have now settled down into the understorey for the night. I continue on, arms flailing, adding to my building sweat.

To the south of the Knott, I stop awhile to watch what I think is a red admiral butterfly flying to and fro in a small clearing on the path. We two remain like that for minutes, and I stand still while the butterfly flits erratically around me, purposefully skimming my head from time to time. And then, he or she is gone, and I am left alone. Just me and the heat.

At the southern edge, the spray of flowers has wilted and now looks rather sad beside the hollow stump. I spot a further butterfly, flying in and out of a dense patch of brambles, and I move closer to investigate. In waiting for a photograph opportunity, I feel a sharp pain on my calf and quickly swipe away a nasty horsefly, only for it to settle immediately on my other calf and begin biting again. They are nothing if not determined and persistent. I have had enough and move on.

I check the five-bar gate for dragonflies, but there are none yet. The dense bracken in the parkland is head height and the oaks are magnificent in leaf. The ruin of the Dower House is painted orange in the sunset light. I turn right off the main track and head up the slope to join the path that runs parallel to the main track for some time, heading due north. I catch glimpses of the flickering lowering sun through the trunks ahead.

There is less understorey growth in the eastern part of the wood (why is that?), and so my friends the flies have departed, at least for now. I pass an area where selective felling has taken place; lengths of timber and piles of scrub and branches are spread neatly over the woodland floor. A reminder that the wood is actively managed. It does no harm.

I eventually drop down to the main track and follow it a little way, heading in the direction of the arch, before turning left, heading west and in the direction of the small wooden footbridge. I am quickly reacquainted with my companions, the flies. They keep me company until I am back out into the pasture.

The orange sun sits just above the treetops on the close horizon, and the square tower of the church is silhouetted between the canopies ahead.

It has only cooled a couple of degrees by the time I am back at the car, and it will prove to be a hot and uncomfortable night.

THIRTY-TWO
OF THE WOODPECKER

Sunday, 4 August 2019 – 05.45

It is light when I leave the car at the start of the track to the arch. Over my left shoulder, the early sun has just broken the horizon formed by the hills north-west of Newnham. All is quiet and still. I pass to the side of the arch into the cool and shade of the wood and turn immediately left, along the old way running parallel to the northern edge and heading due east.

The sun shines low below the canopies, painting shafts of golden early light across the woodland floor ahead of me. The route to the five-bar gate is largely uneventful apart from the fleeting glimpse of a muntjac and perhaps a distant glimpse of the white rump of a roe a long way ahead. There are more fungi to photograph for the later chapter, including good-sized bracket fungi stepped up the white trunk of one of the few silver birch present in the wood.

As nearly always, the wood and its margins are filled with birdsong and call this early Sunday morning. I can hear jackdaw, pheasant and tits and the laugh of the woodpecker.

As I make my way along the southern edge, brushing myriad unseen silken threads from my face, the woodland path skirts very close to the parkland, so much so that my passage disturbs birds foraging in the grasses in amongst the head down sheep. At one particular point, I disturb a couple of woodpeckers who both take flight into the morning air; one heads out into the parkland with its looping flight in search of a quieter place to forage, perhaps in search of paddock ants around the numerous ancient grassy mounds, but its friend lands on a visible branch on a nearby oak. I do not think he or she has spotted me, so I stop awhile to watch with the aid of my monocular.

The woodpecker is a reasonable size, somewhere between a blackbird and a jackdaw and has dull green plumage to its back and speckled plumage to its chest. Despite the absence of a red head (or maybe it is just the light), I think it is a very young green woodpecker. I watch while it preens itself in seemingly impossible contortions. Its most distinguishing feature, and one I had no idea about, is its tongue of disproportionately long length. The woodpecker flicks out its tongue snake-like, almost as if tasting the air. I shift position slightly, and this is enough to attract the woodpecker's attention and to cause it to move on, out of sight.

Just beside the stump of the Great Beech, and in a lofty position, is a patch of flowers at the top of tall stems. The leaves are long, perhaps fifteen to twenty centimetres, and lance shaped with wavy edges. The leaves, arranged in opposing pairs, are a woody dark green with a noticeable, much lighter thick vein along the centre, running from base to tip. The flowers, towering above me, are a dazzling purple and form a conical cluster at the top of the individual plants. Each flower has five unequal flowers and noticeable stamens. I know the plant to be rosebay willowherb (*Chamerion angustifolium*), which is a perennial, flowering from June through to September. Another British name for rosebay willowherb is 'bombweed' as the plant was quick to establish itself on bomb-damaged ground in the Second World War.

I drop down from the southern edge and head in the direction of the Knott, but instead of making the climb, I take the lesser path to the left, in an attempt to retrace my steps along the newfound path recorded a few entries ago.

On my way, I spot a plant that is abundant in the wood. I have been waiting for it to flower for a while. Each side of the path ahead of me is flanked and defined by the plants now in flower. The plant stands around forty to fifty centimetres high. The leaves, around seven to ten centimetres in length, are oval shaped and lightly sawtoothed to the edge and arranged in opposing pairs. The stem of the plant is noticeably hairy. The flowers are asymmetrical in shape with one large greeny white petal at the top, with a whiter petal below in a vague 'm' shape. The heart of the lower petal is purple, with yellow at the very centre. The flowers are less than a thumbnail in size. According to the now well-thumbed field guide, I think it is common hemp-nettle (*Galeopsis tetrahit*). It is an annual and flowers between June and September. A little further on, I find examples of the same plant but this time with a pinky white flower with yellow centre.

I continue on, avoiding encroaching bramble and nettle threatening to choke the path and making me wish that I had worn longs. The way ahead is blocked by a tangled mass of fallen oak branch in full leaf and really more like half the tree, rather than a single branch. Already, a bypass is clearly visible over the woodland floor where other walkers have had to detour. I take a while to study the lichens in different shades of yellows and greens on the mass of fallen branches and decide again that there lies further material for another chapter.

A short while later, I pass by the deeply fissured bark of a dead sweet chestnut, the bark already starting to fall away in places at the base. I gaze up at the radiating skeletal arms high above me; they reach out from the barkless trunk as if to push back the foliage looking to encroach on the recently created break in the enclosing canopy. The uppermost bare branches are painted in golden sunshine.

I pass young oaks bearing young acorns and sycamores with unripened helicopters, both a hint that autumn is now only a couple of weeks away. With thoughts turning to the end of the year, I wander the paths mostly at random but generally heading north. Eventually, opting to head out by the meadows rather than by the arch, I leave the comforting confines of the wood.

The mown pasture is no longer the rich wonder of vibrant life that it was only a couple of entries ago, and I am saddened. A solitary gatekeeper flutters erratically over the dew-soaked grass.

I stick to the meadow all the way to Chapel Lane. Just before the kissing gate exiting onto the lane, I marvel at a miniature enchanted forest of many bonnet-capped white and grey toadstools growing close to the base of an oak. Nature is surprise and wonder, and my spirits are lifted as I make my way up the lane to the car.

THIRTY-THREE

OF THE SWEET CHESTNUT

Thursday, 15 August 2019 – 19.30

Last weekend was busy and a trip up the wood impossible. I had also intended a midweek visit but the M6 traffic had other ideas. Never mind; here I am, on the track up to the arch in the relative cool of the evening. It looks as though I may have the wood to myself.

The acres of barley in the fields either side are yellowing and must be nearly ready for the harvest. I pass tall grasses gone to seed and lower down, dead nettles in white flower. The bright red poppies on the field margins nod rhythmically to and fro in the breeze, their paper-thin petals fluttering. All comforting signs of an English high summer.

The dark mass of the wood stretches out before me, and I welcome its familiar embrace. I have promised not to be too long this evening and decide on taking the main track, which splits the wood very roughly in half.

I have not ventured far in before I hear the 'kewick' of a female tawny owl close by to my left, really just off the path and up in the canopies overhead. And as I stop to listen, and turn in the direction of the owl, a doe emerges gracefully from the understorey onto the path a short way behind. But with a glance at me, she is gone with purpose, quickly across the path and back into the dark of the wood on the opposite side. I wish I could tell her that I mean her no harm.

The fruits of the rambling bramble beside the path are turning that deep purple black, but they are not yet ripe – it will not be long though.

I approach the five-bar gate carefully. As I arrive, I catch a glimpse of the dark, striped tail of what might be a hare disappearing between the bracken – it was large enough and with the arched back and characteristic loping gait. If it was a hare, it is probably the first time I can remember seeing one up the wood. I stop just a little while, leaning on the gate for support, and watch, contented (no bats, no dragonflies). This is definitely my thinking spot and as familiar for me as my own lounge. I could just stop and watch for a lifetime. Jackdaws skirt across the late evening sky and over the top of the sentinel oaks in their tens and twenties, chatting to each other and getting ready for the roost before dark.

We have had unseasonably high winds recently, and evidence of this can be seen all-round; battered green leaves lay untidily strewn over the ground, fallen before their time. In amongst the leaves are twigs and branches and early fallen immature sweet chestnuts (I wonder what the harvest will be like this year?).

I have said that I would bring you descriptions of the trees that, after all, are what makes the wood, the 'wood'. Sweet chestnut (*Castanea*) is prevalent in the wood and probably makes up around ten to fifteen per cent of the tree species. It grows to around thirty-five metres in height at full maturity and can live for up to six hundred years. The bark on an older tree has an almost sculptured architectural appearance, comprising deep fissures arranged in a vertical spiral pattern, reminiscent of moulded church pillars. The leaves have a long, oval shape with heavily sawtoothed edges. The mature leaves have a deep, glossy green appearance in spring and summer and can grow up to twenty-five centimetres in length. The leaves turn a yellow-golden colour in the autumn and are a picture. They fall in dense mats to cover the woodland floor. It is around the same time that the spikey, cased fruits fall to be gathered and consumed by hungry squirrels and humans alike. Some years, the fruits are fat and produce a good harvest; other years, they are barely worth gathering.

The sweet chestnut is not native but was introduced by the Romans as a food source. I guess the legionnaires may have even ground dried chestnuts to produce flour for baking. There are both mature examples and young sweet chestnut trees in the wood, which must be 'self-set'. Sweet chestnut can be coppiced; that is to say that periodically, before maturing, and around every twelve or so years, the wood can be harvested and the straight poles used for fencing (paling). There are many multi-stemmed mature sweet chestnuts up the wood, and I think it is clear that at some point they must have been harvested for their poles, but I wonder how long ago?

I continue on along the southern edge, dodging around a large fallen oak branch, and spot a broad-leaved helleborine – not just the one, then.

At around the same spot we observed the woodpecker in the last entry, my attention is caught by a cock pheasant pecking in amongst the grasses out in the parkland and around the base of an oak, initially oblivious to my presence. But then, he spots me and comically stoops down low and creeps – chest low, slowly but purposefully – out of view, satisfied that, to him at least, he has remained invisible.

I eventually find myself heading up the southern slope of the Knott. The sun is a bright gold disc glimpsed between the miles of trunks ahead to the left. On the way down the other side, heading north, the path has been smoothed in long, wavy tracks where run-off from the recent storms has energetically flowed down the Knott's relatively steep slopes, sweeping away the leaf litter to reveal the hardpacked earth.

There are fungi to be seen everywhere, and much of my time is spent on hands and knees to get a good photo for identification – there are browns, reds, golds and blues.

I pass the converging streams and briefly check on the plants in the marsh but still no flower. I am beginning to think that we will not see them in flower this year.

I leave the wood via the arch and out into the open, into the evening and before the gloaming. The breeze has dropped, and all is still and quiet.

THIRTY-FOUR
OF THE GUELDER ROSE

Sunday, 18 August 2019 – 14.15

It is Sunday afternoon. After a day and a half of intense DIY, I need a break. Despite invitations, I have myself for company. I park up in the greens and head for Brookside Lane.

Growing on the bank of the young Nene, I spot bright red berries growing at the top of a short green stem, against the backdrop of dark green ivy leaves, spread out over the sloping bank. I know the plant to which the berries belong instantly – they are the fruits of lords and ladies, the distinctly tropical-looking plant we observed back in the spring. The berries are a bright orangey red and formed in a tight bunch.

I continue on along the lane and then into the shade of the narrow path winding its way between laurel and the yews of the burial ground to my right. A short time later, I emerge into the full sun washing over the lower pasture. The grass remains uncut here. It is not long before I spot a dragonfly (the first of many today), but it is too quick for identification.

As I often do, I wonder what I shall see today. Shall I have enough to write about and hold your interest? My thoughts are interrupted by the clock at Badby church striking half past the hour. I reach the upper pasture, through the kissing gate, which clangs carelessly shut behind me, loud enough to wake the adjacent dead. Thistle seeds fill the air, carried on the wind and blown rapidly over the pasture. As a backdrop to the wood, angry clouds scud across the sky. In the distance, a lone buzzard circles gracefully over the wood, silhouetted black against the grey cloud.

As I drop down over the ridge, with the grassed slope before me down to the northern edge, I disturb a foraging carrion crow; he takes flight and glides without effort low over the down sloping pasture below me and in the direction of his wood refuge. I watch. The sun turns his glossy black feathers bright silver for a short time, before he is lost in amongst the dense green canopies.

I enter the wood and, turning immediately right, following the path skirting the northern edge. The gusty wind, impotent down here at ground level, is blowing hard and noisily in the leafy canopies above me.

I notice on the woodland floor ridged green fruits, no more than a couple of centimetres across in size. They are alien-looking and sticky to the touch; I suspect I know what they are – I think it is another type of gall. According to the guide, it is a knopper gall, produced in the same way that the marble galls are on our young oak in an earlier entry. The knopper gall is the product of the *Andricus quercuscalicis* gall wasp, which, through the laying of an egg in the young acorn, has caused it to mutate – the more eggs laid, and larvae hatched, the greater the distortion, until the original acorn is barely recognisable. The knopper gall only forms on pedunculate oak, the wood's predominant oak species.

On reaching the confluence of the streams, and on a whim, I decide to follow the stream north-west to see where it takes me. Off path, the going is fairly OK, although a little bit of a scramble. I duck under entwined masses of honeysuckle and over low branches. I come across a mature oak, recently wind fallen, its buttress roots exposed and the earth where it once proudly stood freshly disturbed. I walk along its horizontal length, over rough, textured bark and around branches laid low and then up – or rather along – into the still leafy canopy, now spread out in disarray over the woodland floor. I jump down and backtrack to the stream.

The way ahead is blocked by dense bramble and understorey growth, so I cut across the stream to the other side; I am not the only one to have done this; the opposite bank is exposed mud, where myriad other beasts have made the crossing. Cloven hoof prints of the deer are clearly visible.

I continue following the stream this time, now to my left. I enter a space, in amongst the trees and well off the path, that is a different world, where I am an interloper. An avian world. The call and song of the birds is a pleasing cacophony all-round me – calls that I recognise belonging to the blue tit and great tit and the song of a solitary robin. But there is another call I do not recognise – it is repetitive and shrill, belonging to a slightly more elusive bird. I stand still, watching as a pair, or maybe more (it is hard to tell), flit frenetically from trunk to trunk and branch to branch. The chest plumage, from a distance, has a salmony pink hue, with darker plumage to the wings. It is an agile and small compact bird, with stumpy robust tail and overall sleek appearance – I think it is a nuthatch (the field guide confirms). They are noisy and busy, and honestly, I could watch them all day, but I have to keep going.

I leave that avian world behind me, bearing a broad smile. I continue on, along the right bank of the stream, before it becomes little more than dispersed flow over the woodland floor. Eventually, the steam returns to a defined banked course, clear water washing over the orange clay where the stream enters the wood from the pasture beyond. I spot another broad-leaved helleborine, this time gone to seed.

A little further on, and I have cause to stop again – not far away, within metres, a robin redbreast is perched proudly on the uppermost exposed root of a fallen sycamore, singing for all he is worth. And by reply, I can hear the same song from another robin behind in the distance, calling out his territory. I know the robin to be very territorial and will fiercely defend its territory, even to the death. And beware, folklore has it that to disturb a robin or its nest will surely bring bad luck.

After a time and a little wandering, I find myself at the rhododendron glade, all trace of flowers gone. The bracken, which after appearing to grow a foot or more between each visit, and reaching over head height at its peak, is now a dense tangled mat of plants little more than thigh high. This space is ablaze with sunshine, under a deep blue cloudless sky. But I am not alone; dragonflies, maybe five or six in number, criss-cross the confines of the glade above and around me. They pass close every now and then, and I hear the gentle clatter, and sometimes thrum, of their wings. I watch one; its 'hawking' pays off and it catches a smaller flying insect on the wing, caught in the dragonfly's distended legs. It moves on, feasting on the wing.

Eventually, I find myself walking through the grove of firs

north of the Knott. The air is heady with the clean smell of pine, and I spy more fungi to record. As I emerge out of the shadow of the firs and onto the path following the southern edge, I am greeted by a solitary vocal schnauzer announcing to his family that there is a stranger ahead. When they catch up, we exchange 'hellos' and agree that schnauzers are born noisy. For a time, the exchange brings pleasant memories of walks with Dad and Ollie. Dad was not generally fond of dogs, but he warmed very quickly to Ollie and his endless fun.

Lost in thought, I arrive in no time at the five-bar gate. Still no dragonflies to be seen; I think it is too windy. I head north along the main track, uncertain of which way to head back to the car. When I reach the main crossroads, I turn left as if heading for the Knott (all paths lead to the Knott!) but then strike right along the trail of a lesser path. After not very long, the path, which was not especially well defined to begin with, has petered out, and I find myself carefully making my way through bramble and nettle. But I persevere, and very soon my bare shins and calves are buzzing. I eventually join another path, one I do not recognise but heading north and running parallel to the main track, which is somewhere off to my right.

The path takes me past the title of today's entry; it is a shrub, a little straggly, by reason of adjacent growth and competition for space. Its leaves have an acer shape, being three lobed with slightly toothed edges; the leaves are arranged in opposing pairs and are slightly smaller than my hand. If it was not for the berries, I would think it *was* an acer. The berries are yellowy red and (presumably) unripened but destined for deep red. The berries group in clusters at the end of the branches. The berries mean that it cannot be an acer, and according to the field guide, it is a guelder rose (*Viburnum opulus*) and I think probably the only one of its kind in the wood. The guelder rose grows to around four metres in height and is a tree, rather than a shrub. The flowers are white and form in clusters. According to the guide, it is widespread in woodland up to southern Scotland. It is however a new species for me and a welcome discovery.

The remainder of my walk back to the northern edge is uneventful but otherwise very pleasant. The last observation for the day is a rather uninspiring plant, a bit tatty and overlooked but probably familiar to us all. At school sports days, waiting between events, you would probably have picked the stalks and leaves of this plant and pulled out the 'veins'. The leaves are oval to spherical in shape, arranged in a circle around the stem, dark green in colour with a slightly leathery texture and deeply veined. The flowers are basic and comprise a prominent spike with very small, often brown, protruding flowers. The plant is greater plantain (*Plantago major*), and according to the guide, grows between ten and forty-five centimetres in height (that must just be the flower spike) and flowers from June to October.

Greater plantain grows pretty much anywhere, but the specimen I have spotted is in the upper pasture – Greater plantain does also grow in the wood. Other names for greater plantain include 'rat tail' (reference to the flower spike) and 'waybread'. Greater plantain has long been used for treating sores and ulcers, hence its other name 'soldier's herb'.

The haws, sloes and crab apples grow fat in the hedgerows.

THIRTY-FIVE

OF THE HARE

Saturday, 24 August 2019 – 05.50

It promises to be a fine late summer day and our Welsh adventure beckons. But I have managed to sneak in a quick last-minute wood visit before our journey to the Llyn Peninsula, to the backdrop of sleepy mutterings of 'you really ought to pack the car, you know'.

I make my way under a typical summer sky to the wood edge and before long, lost in thought, I am deep within the cool of the interior, off path, rising up through mast-straight pines, treading lightly through scrub and over long felled criss-cross trunks. Placing steps carefully over the needle-strewn ground. My efforts are futile as always; a jay complains harshly at my ever-unwelcome intrusion from his lofty position out of sight in the dense evergreen canopy overhead.

I continue to wander, avoiding larger obstacles, dismissing

the last vestiges of pre-holiday work thoughts that continue to probe and intrude into a wood state of mind.

My aimless wanderings give way to a well-trodden path as the pines transition gradually to the high beeches. I am surprised out of conflicting daydreams by a loping creature, brown and gangly. He stops, settling on haunches, long, large ears erect. Seemingly saucer-sized eyes regard me, not twenty yards away on the path ahead. Unconsciously, my breath is held, chest at rest, and we gaze upon each other. And I wonder if this is not the same hare glimpsed out in the parkland not long ago.

We both remain still, giving away no movement, but he is no fool. He lifts his angular brown head, twitching nose to the air, scenting my presence. And then, in a lithe twist of his body, he is gone and lost beyond the rise in the path. I follow, reaching the top of the shallow rise where I find that he has merged effortlessly back into cover. Another special moment.

But the hare carries superstition weightily on his arched back. They have a long association with the mischief of hags and witches, and I wonder at the portent of our lone meeting out here on the paths of the wild wood.

THIRTY-SIX

OF THE TAWNY OWLS

Sunday, 25 August 2019 – 19.50

I am on holiday again while I write this entry.

I am sat on the wooden bench outside our tiny low-eave and typically Welsh grey slate cottage. It is very quiet, apart from the birdsong and deep croak of a nearby raven. The domed mass of Garn Boduan dominates the vista to the north.

To the wood.

Jim Bob and I park up in the greens and head in via Brookside Lane. It is close to sundown. The gardens backing onto the brook are filled with idle talk and laughter on this very warm bank holiday weekend. The lower pasture has now also been cut, and Imogen passes comment on the absence of flowers and insects. I tell her that they will be back next year, and the cutting of the grass partly helps with that cycle.

The wood is very quiet, apart from distant calls of crows chatting before the night. It is not full dark inside the wood, but it is not far away. We pass a honeysuckle in nearly full flower and the late evening air is filled with its sweet fragrance. Imogen takes a photograph of a single honeysuckle flower, captured dazzling white in the camera flash against a black background. She is my avid assistant.

Imogen hears a cricket in the grasses deep within the wood. I rely on her to point their chirruping out to me now; I appear to have lost that particular range of my hearing. We arrive at the Knott after a steady climb up the northern slope. We are too early for the badgers but not too late for a solitary dragonfly hawking within the clearing at the top. I lay down on my back on the dry, short grass, hands laced behind my head, and watch the stealthy black silhouette against the dark blue sky, tracking backwards and forwards and criss-cross.

We are losing the light all the time as we head down the southern slope with the firs to our left.

I mentioned early on in this journal that we might get to speak with the owls. I knit my fingers of both hands and press my thumbs together side by side, leaving a thin slit between. I then place my top lip over the knuckles of both thumbs, rest my bottom lip over the formed opening and blow, tentatively. Trying as best as I can to mimic the call of the male tawny owl. After a few fumbled attempts, and some laughter from the daughter, I hit the sweet spot. And by reply, we can hear the 'kewick' of a nearby female tawny owl and, shortly after, the distant 'hoot' of a male tawny owl. The female draws nearer to our spot, before moving further away and eventually falling silent. We continue to speak with the male though, and he hoots in reply for a while. Imogen, although patiently indulging my eccentricities, is keen to move on.

We find ourselves at the five-bar gate as you know we often do. The cloudless dark blue sky is punctuated by a single bright planet hanging loftily above the sentinel oaks in the parkland. We watch as the bats use the space above our heads between the trees of the main track as unhindered passage into and out of the wood. I am struck by how it is not just us humans that use the wood's pathways for transit.

We make our way back along the main track, walking beneath a tree-framed avenue of sky darkening to gloaming blue.

THIRTY-SEVEN

OF THE RAVENS

Saturday, 31 August 2019 – 14.30

I have decided on a different route into the wood today, one we have not fully described before. I have just dropped Em off; she is waitressing at a wedding at the Hall, just a stone's throw away.

I park up, off the road. The lichen-encrusted walls and crenelated tower of the Church of St Mary the Virgin, standing proud in the parkland, are just visible through the trees edging the lane. I am using the final leg (dependent on where you start) of the Knightley Way to access the wood this afternoon, fresh back from Wales not two hours before.

I pass through the kissing gate leading into the expanse of Fawsley parkland. The landscape slopes upwards away from me, interspersed with veteran oaks and the odd veteran beech.

In-between these carefully positioned sentinels are dotted sheep, freshly sheared, and young trees protectively enclosed by fencing. The young trees appear to be a part of a concerted effort to restore the parkland by the estate. The wood is out of view at this point, hidden behind by the rising land to the north.

The sunshine is broken by remnant grey cloud; amorphous shadows flow steadily over the rolling landscape, hugging contour and shallow valley. In the sky to my right, Bran, black against blue, soars on the breeze, letting out his guttural croak. He is flying due north over the rising ground and on the way to the wood. I have not seen or heard from him for a while and for a time he reminds me of the holiday.

I continue on and am beginning to catch up with three fellow walkers ahead. As I near the top of the long slope, where the land begins to level off, there is an ancient oak to the left of the path. Today, sheep stand below its spreading leafy boughs, in the shade, and watch me warily as I pass. At the base of the oak, the buttress roots are exposed through the actions of rabbit and his friends, aided by the forces of the weather. The exposed roots form dark arches and miniature caverns below the mass of the trunk. The exposed tangle of roots reach down deep into the orangey soil to ensure strong purchase. I have known this tree most of my life; I have always thought that this tree, this lofty spot, would have been perfect for Hazel and his friends. The sheep continue to watch as I pass.

I reach the other walkers and we exchange pleasantries as we always do, away from the pavement and our busy lives.

The wood is now visible in front. I enter through the southern edge. There is a kissing gate here – the avenue of Badby Down tapers away to my left. The narrow path drops down into the wood between a dense tangle of elder and bramble. The elder has an unfortunate reputation as a weed of the hedgerow and wood. It is fair to say that it is not one of our more graceful or majestic trees, having a rather untidy, haphazard appearance, and it is often really little more than a big shrub. But I think it is versatile and a survivor.

I know from experience that elder, even when rigorously attacked, will very quickly spurn forth fast-growing straight shoots if you happen to turn your back, even if only for a short while. Its leaves, ovate in shape and sawtoothed edged, are arranged in pairs with a terminating central leaflet. We had an elder in the paddocks at our home in New Zealand whose bark was deeply fissured with age. Every spring, we would gather the white flowers to make elderflower champagne, and in the autumn, the elder produces clusters of deep maroon berries feasted upon by blackbirds. We have not experimented, but the berries can be used for making wine and sauces.

I remember from my childhood Dad showing me how to carve and peel the bark of the young straight stems of the elder into geometric patterns. I guess he would have done the same when he was a kid. In amongst the untidy elder, the blackberries grow fat beside the path and the wood has that rich, earthy smell from the recent rains, and the breeze brings down drips and drops to patter all around me.

I take the path along the southern edge, heading west, passing through beds of healthy-looking wood sorrel. I pass through the damp rhododendron glade and on the edge, spot a young oak in acorn. Its wet leaves are a rich, almost metallic dark green in contrast to the paler yellow-green of the acorns. Before very long, I decide to head off the path and head due north, dropping down the steady slope into the heart of the wood, between and around the trunks, and through the bracken. There is a wren ahead, complaining vocally at my intrusion into its world. I watch him, watching me, at least until he disappears into the bracken, still complaining as he goes.

I continue on, and a short way ahead, I pick up a ride through the wood: a clear, grassy break between the trees but little used by us humans, being away from the network of paths. The ride is soft underfoot, and I stop to inspect the myriad cloven hoof prints of the deer – both roe and muntjac – that clearly use the ride regularly on their wanderings within the confines of the wood. Their tracks are easy to spot, and I follow them for a while.

I spot common figwort now gone to seed; for most, the business of growing is nearly done, and energy is now focused on seed and fruit production, to ensure succession. I eventually join a more formal path and pass the fallen oak branch mentioned a few entries back, its leaves now brown and dead, an afront to the world of green around it. I head off path again back up the slope and find myself with the earthen terraces of the southern sett ahead of me, its occupants tucked safely away from the light and activity of the day. A short distance to the east of the sett, I pass the large patch of foxglove rosettes spotted many entries ago; I was wrong, some are still in late purple flower, but this patch will be a picture in spring and summer next year. Although professing to know the wood as well as anyone, for a while I am disoriented and not able to recall whether my exit back into the parkland lies to my right or my left, but after doubling back, I leave the wood via the Knightley Way back into the sun-washed parkland.

As I take the long slope down to the car, Bran is joined by his partner, and I stop to watch as they perform an aerial ballet, calling to each other. It turns out I have three books on British birds in my collection (you cannot really call it a library

– they are spread all over home), but not one mentions the raven. I know them to be the biggest of our 'blackbirds' whose relatives – the corvids – include rook, carrion crow, jackdaw, jay and magpie. Ravens mate for life and are often seen in pairs. I observed on holiday that when flying, their wings produce a distinct whooshing noise. The raven does not deserve its rather ominous reputation as a harbinger of doom, perpetuated by many authors:

> And the Raven, never flitting, still is sitting, still is sitting
> On the pallid bust of Pallas just above my chamber door;
> And his eyes have all the seeming of a demon's that is dreaming,
> And the lamp-light o'er him streaming throws his shadow on the floor;
> And my soul from out that shadow that lies floating on the floor
> Shall be lifted – nevermore!

The Raven (excerpt)
Edgar Allen Poe

That is the end of August and the end of our time in the Summer Wood. Now into the Autumn Wood and the steady progression to the end of our journey.

PART FOUR
AUTUMN WOOD

THIRTY-EIGHT
OF THE MUNTJAC

Thursday, 5 September 2019 – 19.20

Into the Autumn Wood. Only, the foliage is still that rich summer green, but is there just a hint of autumn chill in the air? I am on the main track, passing dead nettles and poppies still in flower. A half-moon shines bright over the wood in the last light of the day and in a cloudless evening sky.

The dog rose growing by the side of the track is festooned with rosehips. I know from previous reading that the rosehips of the dog rose and its close relatives can be gathered and processed to make rosehip syrup, a good source of vitamin C. When my father-in-law worked at the local infant school in my hometown, he came across a school ledger detailing pupil absence from the early 1900s, and one of the reasons for mass absence given at this time of year was for 'berry picking in the hedgerows. I feel sure that as well as blackberries, elderberries and perhaps sloes, the children would also have gathered rosehips for making syrup. It is a shame that by and large we have lost that connection with the plentiful free food available on our doorstep. And in doing so, we are also that much more detached from the seasons and the changes that they bring.

I enter the still wood and, on a whim, head down a less used path heading south-west – its way choked every now and then by bracken and bramble. It is not long before I cause two deer to take flight; they are just a fleeting glimpse of brown and white between the trunks. After a while, and not far from the painter's crossroads, there is a loud and harsh bark from behind me, nearby. Is there just a small primeval fear response there for a second, something triggered from deep down and from a time before? It certainly made me jump. The first bark is followed closely by a second, slightly further away. And now, I am intrigued. If it is the fox, then it is the first time I have heard its bark since way back at the beginning of the year. But it did not sound quite right. I stop in my tracks, curiosity getting the better of me, and turn to follow. I walk carefully off the path, over the leaf litter and avoiding twigs, trying to be quiet but with little success. The barks continue at regular intervals, and I draw nearer. Before long, I spot the source of the bark, not too far ahead, stood stock still, watching, listening, alert. It is a surprise – not a fox at all but a muntjac, and maybe one of those I had disturbed earlier. For a few moments, we hold each other's gaze, but then, with a flash of bright white tail, it is gone, merging with the dark browns and greens of the wood.

I give up the chase, my curiosity quenched, and head due north and, after a steady climb and in the failing light, arrive at the sett close to the summit of Knobbly Knott. It is still too light for the badgers, but they will be stirring from their slumber.

I remain off the path and battle through the thigh-high bracken and bramble, passing below the canopy of the solitary horse chestnut now laden with fattening conkers. I drop down the southern slope and nearby, the tawny owl is very vocal again, calling to the approaching night from the grove of firs to my left. And the crows and jackdaws are raucous in the treetops.

The waxing moon maintains her vigil over the wood as I head back to the car.

THIRTY-NINE

OF THE SYCAMORE

Saturday, 7 September 2019 – 15.00

I have a new and welcome introduction for this entry: my eldest, Will. He was, or is, at a loose end this Saturday afternoon and has joined me for this trip up the wood. It has been a while. I want to show him Brookside Lane and the view of the wood from the upper pasture, and so we head in that way.

In the upper pasture, all is quiet, and we stop awhile in our lofty position to admire the sweep of the wood. Will has not seen the wood from this position before, and he is impressed. The wood remains a dark band of green.

A solitary, small moth flitters about nearby, just above the now short grass. It alights long enough for me to take a photograph – wings splayed out wide, silvery white and speckled with light greys – in scale effect. Its hairless antennae extend outwards either side of the arthropod's head and are nearly as long as its forewings. Its abdomen protrudes noticeably beyond the trailing edge of its rear wings. Despite my field guide, this one has me flummoxed. It could potentially be the puss moth (lovely name), but that species has hairy antennae and is bigger, I think.

We continue dropping down the slope to the northern edge, and once within, we head right, following the northern edge, heading west. I make one last final, final check on the plants within the marsh but still no flower. I think Will is amused.

It is sunny and warm, and I know the rhododendron glade will be a picture, so we head that way, talking as we go. I point out paths that we once used when Will was little but which have now fallen out of use, most likely because of a fallen tree or even just a period of non-use at the wrong time of year; nature is quick to expunge our intrusion if left to her own devices. The glade is a pocket of sunshine and circle of blue, broken only by fair-weather cloud. Here be dragons! (This may be my new favourite dragonfly spot in the wood.) We watch two of them hawking within this perfect space, catching acrobatically on the wing. They truly are impressive predators. The dragonflies are joined by a solitary speckled wood enjoying a warm and sunny early autumn day. It is settled on a lime green bracken stem, wings unfolded, angled towards the sun and soaking up the warmth. Our attention is caught by a mewing from above, in our window of sky, framed by the canopies surrounding the glade; first one, then two and finally four buzzards circle and call, rising on invisible columns of warm air.

Will wants to see the Knott, so we head in that direction – it is a wrench to leave the glade though and its ever-changing scene. We spot a further speckled wood on the summit, again enjoying the sunshine. A 'solitary' wasp, more black than yellow, and tiny, moves here and there over the woodland floor in search of who knows what. It is too quick to photograph. And the ants go about their business, while the crickets (Will has confirmed that they are here) chirrup in the long grasses.

Something of the sycamore (*Acer pseudoplatanus*) now to finish off today's entry – there is one to my right now, laden with fruit and looking a little summer worn. Similar to the elder, some label the sycamore as a weed of the wood, but it plays its part, not least anything else, its contribution to the biomass of the wood; I estimate that the sycamore probably makes up around sixty per cent of the wood's tree species. This is no accident; the sycamore is invasive and fast growing and, if left unchecked, will quickly take over as the dominant tree species at the expense of others.

The sycamore can grow to thirty-five metres in height at full maturity, displaying a dome-shaped canopy. Young sycamore has smooth, greyish bark, but with age, the bark becomes deeply fissured and scaly. The leaves are distinct in shape and easily recognisable – they are five lobed with sawtoothed edges, vibrant green in spring, changing to dark green with a generally tatty appearance in late summer. The leaves can grow up to twelve centimetres in length. You will often see black spots on the leaves – these are called tar spots and are caused by a fungus.

From observation, I know that the sycamore flowers in April/May and the flowers are yellow-green in colour and hang in spiked clusters. After pollination, the flowers produce winged fruits, which I have always known as 'helicopters'. You probably already know, but next time you see a 'helicopter' on the floor, pick it up and cast it to the wind, and you will see why the fruit is given that name.

The sycamore is native to mainland Europe but is now

naturalised in Britain. It is thought that the sycamore was first introduced by the Romans (possibly for timber production) or possibly in the Tudor period for the same reason (Woodland Trust). Although invasive, the sycamore is of ecological value, not least its attraction to aphids, which in turn provide a food source for birds and other insects, including ladybirds. I am sure we have all parked under the spreading sycamore and cursed the thousands of dewdrop secretions of the aphid over the polished paintwork of our cars.

The remainder of our trip is unremarkable but pleasant.

FOURTY

OF THE WEASEL

Saturday, 14 September 2019 – 12.30

Will and his friend have asked for a lift to the wood, and having nothing particularly pressing myself, I decide to make a trip of it. I leave them at the chestnut car park and make my way down Chapel Lane. The walk, along a narrow path sitting at the top of a steep bank and elevated above the sunken lane, is pleasant and wooded. The elevated path eventually levels out and I turn left and take the footpath through the pasture to the northern edge.

After the experience a few entries ago in that avian world, my ears are now attuned to the distinctive call of the nuthatch, and I hear the bird nearby soon after entering the wood. I have been thinking for a while that rather than walking the paths through the wood, it would be nice, or rather interesting, to just find a remote spot, sit awhile and see if the wood's creatures come to me, rather than me to them. And in doing so, I might catch them off guard and observe them all the better.

I follow the path along the northern edge for a short while but then turn due south, on the lookout for a suitable remote vigil spot. Ahead I can see a natural depression, dry and leaf strewn but free from bramble. One end is 'bookended' by holly, whose dense, dark green canopy extends down to the woodland floor. I think this is a good spot and settle down on my side but propped up on one elbow. A little adjustment is necessary to remove pointy sticks and a rogue holly branch, but eventually I get comfortable.

I face the sun, bright between the canopies. The woodland floor is a mosaic of light and shade, and the canopies are a canvas of lighter and darker greens. Shafts of sunlight pick out cobwebs and silken threads in dazzling silver. And flying insects are brilliant points of moving light against the darker backdrop.

I take time to observe the trees surrounding me – there is holly, fissured oak and smooth sycamore. To my right is a gnarly and misshapen tree, stunted in height. Its boughs hang over my position, just out of reach. I do not immediately recognise the leaves except to say that they are acer in shape but smaller than the sycamore. I take a photograph and pluck a single leaf for identification for when I get home. Although small, and outcompeted by its towering neighbours, it is clearly of some age.

Minutes pass.

There are periods of rustling and birdsong, matched by periods of stillness and quiet. From time to time I hear human voices, distant and alien. I lay still, pondering on what I might write about today, whether the wood will readily give up its secrets, whether mysteries will reveal themselves. Woodpeckers peck out of sight – always out of sight.

A raven, perhaps Bran, calls from the north beyond the wood margins but draws nearer. The call is frantic and urgent. He passes overhead, glimpsed just briefly; a dark shape seen flitting in open sky through the intertwined network of branches and leaves. He continues calling into the distance.

More minutes pass and Badby church strikes the quarter hour. I remain patient and still.

A robin redbreast alights on a sycamore branch close by. He is unaware of my presence and lets out his territorial song and perches, waiting for reply – there is none. Satisfied, he moves on. Even closer, a nuthatch lands on the trunk of an oak just to my left. It glides effortlessly over the coarse bark, looking for a meal. On the hunt – sometimes sideways, sometimes upside down. A slight movement of my head is enough to send it on its startled way.

A squirrel chatters nearby.

All is still again, and I shift my position slightly to relieve the numbness in my right arm. Badby church strikes the full hour in the distance. There are more human voices, but they pass by, out of view. There is a rustling to my left, very close, just beyond the bank. The rustling gets louder and nearer, accompanied by chattering, and I wait in anticipation for whatever to reveal itself, but initially, I wait in vain. But, after a brief period of quiet, there is an explosion of activity and two squirrels burst forth from the undergrowth to my left, squabbling. They dash in chase across the ground, just in front of my position, at full speed, tails bouncing, kicking up leaf litter, and disappear back into the undergrowth. I cannot imagine that it ends well.

A return to stillness. At least until it turns out that I was not all that remote and hidden after all; three young lads pass close by to my left on bicycles. I observe their passing, but they do not see me. I am reminded of the times my friends and I would cycle out to the wood during the school summer holidays. Badby church strikes another quarter hour and I decide my vigil has been long enough and fruitful. I say farewell to the robin, nuthatch and the squirrels and move on, off path and heading south, steadily up hill. I find a fallen oak, half its roots still buried in the soil and its twisted branches still partially in leaf. I rest awhile on the trunk, but the wood is quiet.

On my way to join Will and his mate, I pass the guelder rose, now laden with bright red berries, and spot a fungus tucked in against the base of an oak. It is large and has the appearance of vertical petals radiating out from the centre – greys and brown on top, with the very edges highlighted in white, with white undersides. The whole fungus is perhaps thirty centimetres across, and it is truly magnificent. We will discover its name at some point.

I leave the wood via the arch and onto the main track. Out in the open, about sixty or so yards from the arch, a weasel (it is too small for a stoat) breaks cover from the knee-high yellowing grasses to my right and not two yards in front of me, crossing the path in a brown streak and entering the ground cover to my left. Gone without trace. Not a single stem of grass is disturbed. This is a first for me, at least up the wood. There is a distinct lack of mention of our smaller mammals and rodents in this journal. We have heard their panicked rustlings at dusk, but they have remained out of sight. So, appropriately, a little about the weasel now.

Weasels are long and thin, enabling them to enter the homes of their prey – rats, mice, voles and young rabbits. Without the tail, weasels range from twenty to twenty-five centimetres in length and their coats are ginger to brown fur on top and white underside, extending up to their throat and pointy features. Weasels are widespread throughout the mainland of Great Britain, but the only time you are likely to be lucky enough to see one is, as today, when they run out in front of you on the road or path.

On my return home, I check my tree guide to identify the tree that I was in the company of earlier; it turns out that it is a field maple (*Acer campestre*). Unlike its cousin the sycamore, the field maple is a native of the British Isles. In the right conditions, field maple can grow to a height of twenty-six metres and has a rounded crown. Its leaves can grow up to twelve centimetres long and have three distinct lobes. My example is rather stunted and consequently its leaves are half that size. The leaves are bright green in spring, turning yellow then reddish brown in the autumn. Field maple flowers in April/May and produces 'helicopters', straighter in form compared to the curved fruit of the sycamore.

FORTY-ONE

OF THE GEESE

Sunday, 15 September – 06.40

It has been a while since I have ventured out on an early morning walk, but the shortening days mean that it is now possible without having to set out too early – it would have been earlier, if not for those extra few minutes in bed. I park up at the chestnut car park. I am not alone, and I glimpse another visitor along the main tack in the distance, surrounded by several excited dogs. We will cross paths later on in the high beeches.

To my left, the sun has broken the horizon but is glimpsed through cloud, stained oranges and reds. To my right, the nearly full moon sits high over the landscape. She is both falling and waning. In the near distance, against the backdrop of the wood, a tired-looking combine stands quiet and idle beside a high-sided trailer. Half the barley is harvested, but more remains to be done. There is a steady cool breeze blowing out of the west, over the cricket pitch. I zip up my fleece to chin to keep out the chill and walk briskly.

I have no objective this morning and meander from east to west through the wood, following lesser paths and sometimes finding dead ends, the way ahead blocked by tangled understorey. Apart from the ever-present bird call, including a single hoot of the tawny owl, there is little to report. I have noticed, which was not all that obvious yesterday, that in places, the leaves of the bramble and other plants are starting to yellow. The blackberries, the majority now fully ripe, provide a good harvest for breakfast. I also pass a solitary elder decorated in dark purple berries.

On my way out, I spot a small shard of Willow Pattern pottery embedded in the compacted earth beside the western buttresses of the arch. It would be entirely out of place if not for the knowledge that squat crenelated gatehouses once abutted each side of the arch.

As I near the car, enjoying the warmth of the risen sun, I hear the unmistakeable call of geese. They emerge out of the east, and out of the glare of the sun, a great flying V and honking in constant chatter. I watch them for a while, stood still on the track, head craned back. They head to my position, before making a near ninety-degree turn south out over the expanse of the wood and presumably on their way to the lakes in the parkland. I watch until they are lost to the horizon.

FORTY-TWO

OF FAREWELLS AND BLACKBERRIES

Friday, 20 September 2019 – 16.10

It is the end of the working week and the end of Em's summer break; she returns to Brighton tomorrow to start her second year. Em is keen for a quick blow around the wood before she returns. It will be a short walk; she has more packing to do. We park up at the chestnuts car park in full sun. The combine, dirty white and green, rumbles away in the field to our left, spewing forth plumes of dust that hang lazily in the still air.

We enter the wood.

Em has not been for a long time, and she observes how dry it is and how the leaves and undergrowth have that tired, late summer look. Drooping, tatty and listless. Vigour and vibrancy gone, at least for this year. We pass a hazel, dwarfed by the surrounding oaks, its uppermost leaves showing the first signs of yellowing. Em informs me, because I did not know, that the chlorophyll present in the leaves of deciduous trees over the spring and summer and an essential part of the trees' conversion of sunlight to energy, breaks down and is reabsorbed by the trees in response to the shortening daylight hours. The reabsorption of the chlorophyll by the tree reveals the autumn golds and reds.

We talk of family matters and the university year ahead and of her new home in Brighton.

We wander below the canopies and along the twisting paths as we talk and the minutes pass. Along the way, we stop often to pick the multitude of blackberries – it is a good year (must remember to bring a bag next time). In our meanderings, which may or may not have taken in the Knott, we pass our 'Christmas tree' and I wonder that it will not be very long before I am back here at this spot soon, as part of our Christmas rituals. A litter further on, and contrary to my earlier thoughts, we walk a path to the east of the Knott which is flanked by a number of guelder rose, in red berry and all twisted and straggly.

We walk beneath sweet chestnuts, the woodland floor below their spreading crowns littered with not-yet-ready prickly and bright luminous green sweet chestnut cases. I wonder why this is. It has not been particularly windy, and therefore I surmise that it could be water stress or maybe the actions of overeager squirrels. Certainly, in places, the cases have been broken open and the unripened white nuts partly consumed. A handy trick for opening the cases, avoiding handling the prickles, is to place the prickly package between your booted feet, whereupon you pinch and prize open the cases with the edge of your soles. As awkward and as unlikely as it sounds, it does work, and Em opens a fallen case, revealing an unripened and bright white tiny chestnut. I am left wondering if this year's harvest will be meagre.

Em says a fond farewell to the wood and comments that the next time she is up, it will be Christmas, when the wood will be a very different place.

FORTY-THREE

OF THE RED KITE

Saturday, 21 September 2019 – 08.00

I have been waiting and hoping for the subject of today's entry. As the months slipped by and the seasons changed, I had thought that the opportunity would be missed, and this journal would be poorer as a result.

I have watched their steady progress and gradual expansion of territory with interest for some time. Beyond the wood and out in the wider area, sightings have been made, and an acquaintance in the village has said that they are visitors from time to time. But today is a first for me.

I make my way along the ever-familiar path and past my portal to the wild. A short and lazy trip today, just to stretch my legs, following my nose. Dawn beasts have retreated to thickets and burrows, making way for human visitors. There is little to report from the wooded confines, as is sometimes the case.

And so, I wander and on unpredictable whims, strike off along paths little used and from time to time break off through scrub and understorey, till my way takes me to the far west side of the wood. There I rest, content to lean on the worn top rail of the fence for a time. About where we were visited by the impatient owl at dusk some time ago.

The view is out over close-cropped field and paddock, with the Down and Plantation beyond. Out in the blue expanse, I settle on a black dot headed my way. I watch its steady and meandering progress. The dot gradually forms the shape of a clear raptor and as it draws near, I spot the distinct forked feathered tail and angular wings. The raptor dips and twists, turning to and fro, sometimes sidewards.

The red kite continues on its flighted path to the wood, and I follow its course in full appreciation, admiring its graceful and sometimes erratic flight. A master of air currents, thermals and eddies of the wind. The red kite is the fighter pilot of the avian world.

He is close now. The subtle red hue of his plumage is clear to see, along with the distinctive white flash towards the underside of the wing tips. And of course, the distinctive 'kite' tail.

He passes nonchalantly overhead and over the sweep of the wood. I catch only fleeting final glimpses between autumn ready canopies, until he is gone. And whilst I could watch for lifetimes, I am left content. When will I see him again, I wonder?

The reintroduction of the red kite is a magnificent success story that I have followed for a long time. Previously long extinct in England, they were reintroduced in the late 1980s in the Chiltern Hills and soon became a regular feature on journeys down the M40. But from my own keen observations, the red kite continues to expand northwards (as presumably to the other compass points from its original Chiltern base) and can now be seen reasonably regularly over rolling Northamptonshire countryside.

To observe the red kite over the wood, previously the reserve of the buzzard and raven, has long been a goal of mine.

It was worth the wait.

FORTY-FOUR
OF AUTUMN SIGNS

Sunday, 22 September 2019 – 10.30

On a whim, I park up in the village, on the green overlooked by the Church of St Mary the Virgin. As I leave the car, the tenor is being raised, so I decide to poke my head into the tower and say hello. After some gentle cajoling, I end up ringing for the second time this morning. Just rounds and call changes. Much else is beyond me at this stage of my schooling.

And so, my walk this morning is delayed, but only ever so slightly, and by eleven o'clock or so, I head down the steep northern slope of the Nene valley on the route of the Knightley Way. I pass by the crab apple, mentioned in an earlier entry, its fruit now fit to bursting, at least some still weighing heavily upon its weeping boughs. The remainder lay scattered and squashed on the narrow, dark earthen path. I make a mental note to ask Mrs Hammond about crab apple recipes when I return home.

Further on, I spot bright red berries hanging suspended from a creeping plant, tangled in the branches of a hawthorn. The berries are that of the bittersweet, that sickly yellow and purply flowered plant we observed back in the spring, and in case you are wondering, the berries are definitely poisonous.

At the top of the far slope, I pass through the kissing gate and out into pasture. The hedgerows to my right and left burst with colourful fruit; rich red rosehips of a rambling dog rose tangled within the canopy of a hazel sit cheek by jowl with dusty deep purple sloes of the blackthorn awaiting the first frosts. A little further on, and beside yet more red-green crab apples, are fat blackberries ripe for picking. I make a further mental note to return here soon and strike off across the pasture. To my left, a little way off, wary sheep lie prone under the low-hanging branches of an ancient hawthorn, its branches too are laden with bright red haws. I leave the sheep to chew the cud and their portent of rain and head for the wooden, smooth, worn footbridge, which is invisible in the dark wall of the wood ahead.

Within the wood, I follow the path down to the confluence of the streams and cross over the first stream and turn right, heading due south. I use the recently fallen oak to cross a deep ditch. Green moist moss is already well established over the now horizontal trunk. On the opposite bank I pass a latrine, located in a shallow depression beside the path. Orangey red flies buzz hungrily around and settle on the black mass. I think it is a badger latrine and more than just a pile of defecation; it is a marker, a message to other badger families. On closer inspection, recent meals appear to have consisted of seasonal berries and grains. Badgers are omnivores, so I see no reason why they should not supplement their normal earthworm diet with some roughage.

I continue on and eventually find myself following the western flank of the Knott, past the tree nursery. The nuthatches, maybe as many as four or five, flit between the canopies and towering trunks of the trees around me. Immediately to my left, a woodpecker goes about his business, hammering on an oak, seemingly hollow, at least that is how it sounds. I move to the base of the oak, just off the path, hopeful of a siting, and gaze up into the canopy high above my head. The woodpecker continues to 'knock'. I do a full circuit of the trunk, moving noisily through dry bracken and leaf litter, enough to silence both the nuthatches and the woodpecker. I move back onto the path, still gazing upwards. A single leaf, autumn gold, high up, twists in a measured downwards spiral through the canopies – the first of many. I watch its steady, perfect progress to the woodland floor and wonder at how we are in autumn already.

Further on, still to the west of the Knott, two jays screech, their unwholesome screech. I think I have said before that there is nothing remotely nice about their call. It is coarse and unfriendly. I know not what they call for; is it me, or are they arguing? I continue on, leaving them to their heated exchange. I pass by a patch of bracken, maybe early growth; it is a collection of yellows and browns, in contrast to the still green bramble.

I turn right, heading west at the base of the hollow way, in the shadow of the Great Beech, and past the patch of still flowering foxgloves. I do not know why I have not consciously noticed it before, but this path – running parallel to the southern edge, high above me to my left – passes through a series of smaller and larger glades of which our rhododendron glade is one. No dragonflies today, but a late speckled wood still flits around and over the bracken.

At the edge of the glade, I pass a young oak, no more than thigh height and crowded by the surrounding bracken, bramble and reeds. Its leaves are a dark, shiny green. I mention this particular oak only because it is in the minority in the wood. It is a sessile oak, whose leaves are quite different from that of the dominant oak species in the wood, that being the pedunculate oak. The sessile oak leaf has a more ordered appearance than the more free-flowing organic leaf of the pedunculate oak, which has fewer lobes. The sessile oak's acorns differ too, being more rounded than the longer acorns of its cousin, and they are also stalkless, growing instead directly against the twig in tight clusters. The sessile oak is more common in the western parts of Britain in hilly areas.

I continue on.

My attention is caught by a glimpse of daylight through an elongated hole in the trunk of an old sycamore, just wide enough to fit my hand up to my palm; the hole is the result of an old scar and internal decay. I wonder whether holes through trees have similar folklore to that associated with holes in standing stones, a passage to underworlds or rites of rebirth? I am always on the lookout for such curiosities of the wood; they are waymarkers and memories. A little further on and I spot another curiosity: a thick vine, snake-like, hugs and is almost at one with its sycamore host and probably just as old – ancient and twisted – its girth nearly a quarter the size of its hapless quarry. The vine twists up and away into the canopy of the sycamore, fanning out Medusa-like in a tangle of lesser woody vines. The canopy is more ivy leaf than sycamore.

I pass quickthorn leaves yellowing and holly in ripening berry. In only a matter of days, the wood and its surroundings are rich in the tentative signs of early autumn.

FORTY-FIVE

OF THE AUTUMN
EQUINOX

Monday, 23 September 2019 – 18.50

Into the murk wood, Jim Bob and I arrive on the edge of the dark.

The drizzle is steady and at times driven by a gusty breeze. Trees sway, their canopies shaken, casting drips and drops.

We walk through puddles on the hard ground. Off the path, either side, the wood fades to darkness; shapes without form and definition. The crows call from their precarious perches and the male tawny owl hoots, far off.

We stop at the five-bar gate for a time, the lighter vista and sky beyond framed by the dark of the canopies. We watch a small black shape perform loops and impossible turns between the sentinel oaks.

The ruined walls of the Dower House stand, stained dark

by the weather. Glassless openings to ceilingless rooms, their occupants long gone, are windows to the darkening sky.

The female tawny owl calls close by from high up in the canopy of an oak in the park. We spy another oak, long dead; skeletal branches reach out, silhouetted jet black against the silver sky.

We turn our backs to the light and move back into the gloomy embrace of the wood; we unconsciously move closer. I am reminded of the words of the painter about how he would not like to be in the wood after dark. We follow the track, more by instinct than sight. Conversation is hushed.

Eventually, the arch emerges from the murk and is a welcome sight. We leave the wild night-time wood into full dark. No stars.

FORTY-SIX

OF WILD WEATHER

Sunday, 29 September – 15.20

The sky is leaden grey, and paler, ragged shower clouds scud with urgency overhead, blown by a strong and gusty westerly wind. Is there just a hint of green fading to soft autumn tones in the expanse of the wood in the distance? As I drop down the steady slope from the upper pasture, and out of the worst of the wind, the leaves of the lower storey of hazels beneath the towering oak and ash on the woodland edge are definitely fading to autumn yellow.

Within the wood, I head east, clockwise, along the northern edge. The wind whips and rattles the treetops and is a constant noisy hiss and rattle through the leaves. It brings down unready leaves and sweet chestnuts; the path before me is an untidy scatter of early autumn debris. I wander up the hill, in solitude. No animal sounds, just the soundscape of the wind.

I continue past the archway in the distance and into the eastern half of the wood. To my left, the foliage of the wood edge is thinning, letting in light and allowing views out over the stubbled field, long since harvested and awaiting the plough. To my right, into the interior, the deep green of the bramble, a dense mat over the woodland floor, is dappled with bright autumn ready yellows. A pine cone cascades down through the leaves overhead and I brace for impact, but the cone lands harmlessly by my feet.

A feature of this part of the wood, before the dense conifers and the meandering climb up into the high beeches, are the dotted wild cherries (*Prunus avium*). Substantial monoliths reach up straight, sharing space with the canopies of the sycamore and oaks. Their bark is distinctive, dark red-brown and shiny and formed in bands encircling the trunk. The veteran wild cherries hereabouts are gnarly at their bases, scarred and fissured, as if the heartwood has outgrown its skin.

Wild cherry is a deciduous tree maturing to thirty metres in height, with a domed crown. Its leaves are ovate in shape; that is to say that they have an elongated oval shape ending in a point. The leaves are around fifteen centimetres long and have forward-facing toothed edges. As we witnessed in spring, wild cherry produces a mass of white blossoms, with each white five-petalled flower being around three centimetres across. The flowers are short-lived, followed after by red cherries that are smaller than the shop-bought variety. The fruit is readily consumed by hungry blackbirds. If you should happen to find a sufficiently ripened cherry that has not been consumed by the greedy blackbird, then you will find it tart to sweet in taste. The wild cherry is widespread throughout the British Isles, except for northern Scotland and western Ireland. A few years back, before NZ, I carefully peeled the upper layer of bark from a wild cherry to make my mate a bark box. He still has the box, and the tree, still standing, is none the worse for wear.

I turn right, taking a path that we used when the kids were young, up through the conifers and in search of stinkhorn fungi. The rather sickly and phallic-looking fungi, white-stemmed and oozy black-capped, grew hereabouts, within the dense shade below the towering pine.

The woodsmen have been busy; mature Scots pine lie in tidy rows on the ground. I stop awhile to count the rings on one of the larger felled trunks. The rings radiate outwards from the core and the gap between the distinctive darker rings closer to the centre hint at frantic growth in the tree's early years, at a time when the young pine was desperate to keep pace with its neighbours. Towards the outer edge, the gap between the rings is markedly less, suggesting a slowing in the pace of growth as the tree matured, having secured its place amongst the constant canopies. I count forty-nine rings in total, one for every year I have been alive. Amazing to think that when Dad first started taking us up the wood, this pine and its neighbours would have been mere juveniles.

Within the pines grows a lone oak, mast-straight with no branches, or at least not until its last few feet way above my head. Competition for light has strongly shaped this peculiar oak, crowded by the pine. There are leaves, but they are bunched in tight clusters on little more than twigs springing forth from the straight trunk.

With no stinkhorn fungi to be found, I move on along a narrow path through a break in the canopies. It is this spot where I observed the mass of foxgloves only a couple of years ago, not long after felling had taken place. There are no signs of foxgloves now (although there must be a substantial seedbank in the ground), and bramble and bracken, and pioneering juvenile birch and hazel, have taken over this space.

The path I am following takes me west of the high beeches, and eventually I drop down to the five-bar gate. A lady, content, sits on a handy stump, legs crossed, gazing out at the parkland. We exchange 'hellos' and I continue on, leaving her to her own wood moment. I take the path just in from the southern edge for a short time but soon turn right, along the eastern edge of the fir grove. I meander through bramble and bracken, and between trunks, ducking under the canopies of low-hung sweet chestnuts, the ground below their crowns littered with green spikey cases and part eaten fruits; I remain sceptical about this year's harvest.

As you know, I am always on the lookout for new fungi to record, and to my left now, a little way off the path, lies a tangled horizontal mass of trunk and branches from a fallen oak. The dark, weather-stained bark has an orange tinge, and I head off path to investigate. From every branch and along the trunk of this once great tree protrudes delicate burnt orange frills growing out horizontally, around two to three centimetres long and wide. The frills are highlighted in bright cream around the edge. I will be writing more about this fungus, and all the others I have recorded, over the last few months, very soon.

I eventually arrive at the Knott and inspect the ground below the spread of the horse chestnut at the top for conkers (it is the season after all), but there are none to be found, just the odd case, which may even be last year's. Is the absence of conkers down to the badgers? The leaves of the horse chestnut have a sick, curled, brown appearance, which I do not think is solely down to the time of year. I have observed in my travels that many horse chestnuts around the Midlands and beyond display the same unhealthy appearance. I wonder whether it is water stress or something more sinister.

I also inspect the oak at the top, healthy and still in green leaf, although clearly feasted upon by an abundance of mini beasts, giving each leaf a delicate filigree appearance. I notice that at the end of each twig, close to the leaf stalks, next year's buds have already formed, waiting for spring.

I drop down the western slope, around and over fallen sweet chestnut trunks and branches. There are still blackberries to be found, but make haste, for today is Michaelmas and according to British folklore, the last day that the blackberry can be safely gathered. On this day, St Michael cast lucifer from the heavenly mount into a patch of bramble, whereupon Lucifer set about the prickly bramble uttering curses, scorching leaf and berry with hellish breath, spitting and urinating until the berries were spoilt.

Aware that I need to make my way out if I am to be home in time for dinner, I take paths heading steadily north. I spot another fallen oak and more photogenic fungi to record. There is one final observation to record from within the wood today; near to the confluence of the streams, a large branch has succumbed to the wind and the wet, maybe even today. The branch has caught a young hazel and bent it double. The hazel's crown is fanned out over the ground. In amongst the leaves, I spot new hazel catkins, little green sausages; they will not open out fully until the spring.

I emerge out of the wind-battered wood and make my way up the slope to the upper pasture. As I reach the high ground, the distant hills to the north are shrouded in the midst of a heavy shower. I hurry for the car.

FORTY-SEVEN
OF VETERANS

Sunday, 6 October 2019 – 15.30

As this journal settles into autumn – when the wood itself starts slowing down to conserve energy in preparation for the long winter and in readiness for the vigour of spring – it is inevitable that holding your interest becomes something of a challenge; after all, the months of frenetic spring growth and rebirth, followed by summer production, all of which are food for words, are now well behind us. So, as is often the case, lying awake somewhere around the witching hour, I have given thought to how I might best add variety. Following on from last entry's observation of tree rings, I thought it would be interesting to try and identify the veteran trees of the wood – those 'old ones' of the wood that have seen centuries pass, oblivious to remarkable events – and to surmise at the oldest of the old.

Before we embark on the hunt, I think it is worth considering for a moment the ways in which we might establish the age of a tree. The obvious method would be to fell so that we might easily count the growth rings, but this is not practical and I suspect would be very unpopular with the land owner. Another way would be to extract a core sample from the tree, but I have neither the tools nor desire to do this for fear of harming the tree. It turns out, though, that there are non-intrusive methods. A Google search reveals a few tree aging methods and pre-populated age measurement tables. After careful consideration, I have decided upon a tree age survey handbook extract produced by Wokingham District Veteran Tree Association. My results recorded later in this entry are based on the Wokingham table.

It is also worth considering those matters and circumstances that influence tree growth and therefore our judgement of age by sight alone. For example, we can look at a mighty oak and beech and judge by sight that they must be many hundreds of years old. And it stands to reason, conversely, that the smaller the tree, the younger it must be in age. But it transpires that that is not always the case.

Peter Wohlleben in his book *The Hidden Life of Trees* observes that a seemingly young beech tree in one of his forests, dwarfed by its neighbours, was actually at least eighty years old. And rather than a one off, further observation confirmed that apparently young trees had already been around for a very long time. But what is the reason for this? As proposed by Wohlleben, the reason is the availability of light; as we have already observed, under the dense mature canopies, light is severely restricted and therefore necessarily restricting growth of the apparent juveniles. That is until such a time as a sudden break in the canopy provides just the right opportunity for vigorous growth. So, the oaks and beeches in our wood may have bided their time over many years, waiting for their moment, before growing to their veteran size we see today.

The most obvious evidence in our wood of the impact of shade on tree growth is visible when observing the sister to the Great Beech. I have mentioned previously that such was the presence and size of the Great Beech that its sister did not waste time or energy on the formation of branches on its eastern flank where light was very limited, and this absence of branches on that side of the tree remains clearly evident today.

It is worth considering for a moment what makes a tree a veteran or indeed ancient. Is there a difference, and is it simply about age, or is it about shape and character? And does the label of veteran or ancient tree change from species to species? Veteran trees are those that might show ancient characteristics, for example wide, hollow trunk and perhaps squat appearance. Ancient trees are simply those trees that are ancient in time, being of great age. The Ancient Tree Forum points out that 'ancient trees are all veterans, but not all veterans are ancient'. And species does make a difference, so for example, birch trees, which are relatively short-lived compared to other species, could be considered ancient at 150 years old, whereas, species that live to great ages, such as oak, may only achieve the accolade of ancient after four hundred or so years.

Enough preamble; let us enter the wood.

I am greeted by a vocal robin as I descend the young Nene valley, and it keeps me company until I leave the intimate confines of the sunken path and emerge out the other side into open pasture. The wind is gusty; not as fierce as the last visit but enough to agitate the still dense wall of foliage in front of me, revealing the silver undersides of fluttering leaves. The paddock is sploshy underfoot, testament to the recent wet weather.

I enter the wood via the wooden footbridge to the raucous complaint of a jay. I pay it no heed and turn right, past hawthorn and sweet chestnut yellowing. Leaves of autumn golds lay scattered, not quite in deep swathes yet, but it will not be long. I continue on, first along the western edge and then the southern edge, following the steadily rising path.

On a fallen trunk, just to the left of the path, there is a fungus – nothing unusual in that; the wood is alive with fungi of all different colours and sizes at the moment, but the most impressive feature of this particular fungus is its great size. Growing out from the top of the long fallen mouldering trunk, the fungus has a span that is forty-four centimetres in diameter. This fungus is like a miniature tree in its own right – a short trunk, rooted in the nutrients of the slowly decaying wood of the tree trunk, supports the massive, mottled canopy, with wavy spread and uneven shape. I am here at just the right time; a couple of days either way and I might well have missed what must be the largest fungus in the wood. Appropriate for the day; I am on the hunt for giants after all. For the record, I think this magnificent giant is perhaps dryads saddle fungus.

I cross over the stream we followed the course of a few entries back, through that avian world. Today, after the rains, the stream babbles pleasantly. Crystal clear water cascades in miniature waterfalls over the exposed Northamptonshire clay. I stop every now and then to capture more photographs of emerging fungi and established lichens of greens, greys and yellows on dark trunks. From one of the clearings, I spot an oak away to my left; high up in the canopy, the odd leaf is showing the first signs of colour.

I continue on.

An abrupt drop in light and rush of wind through the treetops heralds a short, sharp shower. I shelter below the horizontal leafy branches of a young beech, crowding in snuggly to its juvenile trunk, and I wonder how old this seemingly young beech might be, waiting patiently for just the right moment. It will be here long after I am all ash and dust.

A short while later to my left, in the south-western corner of the wood, I spot a likely candidate for a veteran. A magnificent pedunculate oak – straight and solid, with dominant, well-shaped canopy – towers over me as I gaze up into its lofty crown. With a glance around, I remove the tailor's tape measure from my pocket and relieve it of its enclosing elastic band. The wife's words of 'you're not really going to measure trees, are you?' and my boy's single exclamation of 'weirdo' echo fresh in my ears. There is nobody about to observe my rather eccentric undertaking. The oak is on level ground and free of bramble and bracken around its substantial base. I choose a starting point just about my shoulder height and circle the trunk, measuring carefully as I go. A full circuit reveals a girth of 435 centimetres. Based on the Wokingham table, observing the 'within wood' location, the table suggests a potential age of 550 years.

Let us consider for a moment that length of time – a period of over five centuries, spanning the lives of twenty-six English monarchs, beginning before either Henry VIII or Elizabeth I, through countless conflicts, pestilence, disease and famine but also over the time of great works and achievement of human spirit, endeavour and exploration. And it is conceivable that this oak, if favoured by fortune and circumstance, could be around for another five hundred or so years. Is this oak the oldest of old though? I leave the oak behind. I pass swathes of hemp-nettle gone to seed. Where those dainty flowers grew until only very recently, spikey heads now hold small black seeds waiting for dispersal.

Ahead of me, the canopies open up a little and the path runs through a grassy area, within which grow three silver birches, in an evenly spaced row. They have found space to grow and have tidy tapering crowns that are not yet weeping.

On the edge of the next glade, and at the base of the deer bank, I spy a tree out of place amongst the oak and sycamore – it has the appearance of a fir with needled branches dotted with tan-coloured pine cones. The lower branches droop low, brushing the tops of the tired bracken. On consulting the guide, I think it is a common larch. The needles are formed in regular-spaced clusters along the branches and are darkish green in colour. Each cluster produces around twenty-four needles arranged in a radial pattern. Where needles have been discarded, woody nodules remain. I did not know, but according to the guide, common larch is deciduous, and we should see the needles turn yellow soon before they drop. The cone is neat and conical in shape and each scale (if that is what they are called) is rounded. The cone I am observing now on this particular larch must have been there for a little while; green-coloured lichen is forming on the individual scales. I leave the larch and glade behind and continue on, still on the hunt.

I eventually arrive, slightly by surprise (I was following my nose again) at the Great Beech – its sister is also a viable candidate, so I set about with my measuring tape. The beech is on a steep slope which makes measurement tricky, and I wonder how much it might affect the accuracy. But I do the best I can and arrive at a figure for the girth of 354 centimetres. According to the Wokingham table, and having regard to the physical surroundings, the girth suggests an age of around 280 years. I also make an attempt at measuring the girth of the

Great Beech lying prone across the hollow way, but bramble and poor footing prove it impossible (and nearly my undoing). I surmise that it must have the same or greater girth than its sister. As I clamber back down off the ragged horizontal stump, I spot a perfect rusty brown-topped fungus, about handspan in diameter, growing within the enclosure of the hollowed out stump. I leave the perfect fungus behind and head down the steep slope into the heart of the wood.

Knowing the Knott well, there are at least three further potential candidates for the oldest tree, and so I make my way up the southern slope, through the dense bracken and up and over the fallen trunks to the top. The oak at the summit has a girth of 336 centimetres, and having regard to the more open canopy at the top, I estimate an age of around 320 years. Of the two veteran beeches at the top, using the same calculation, I estimate an age of 250 years for the slightly larger of the two, based on a girth size of 320 centimetres.

On the eastern side of the Knott, just down from the summit, are a couple of veteran sweet chestnuts. The largest of the two has a girth size of 413 centimetres, giving an estimated age of 230 years according to the Wokingham table. In my transit around the trunk, I am careful not to disturb a brown-winged moth nestled tight into the fissured chevron bark of the tree.

I continue on down the long eastern slope, before turning right just after the small patch of guelder rose, still in bright red berry. Eventually, after meandering and still on the hunt, I reach the northern edge of the grove of firs. The path to the left is choked and impassable, so instead of doubling back, I cut through the dense shadow of the firs. Not much grows on the floor here.

I have said that I will dedicate a chapter to decay, which I will, but I must mention now a miniature wonder that I have spotted on a ragged stump on my way through the firs. It is a tiny fungus, bright brilliant yellow and spikey, or perhaps better described as horned in appearance – three 'bunches' of the yellow fungus protrude from the moist, red, decaying wood. At the most, the fungus is just five centimetres high, or low! In writing up this discovery – and knowing the name now, which is yellow stagshorn fungus (along with fly agaric, probably the most easily identified fungus out there) – my first impressions of the fungus is that it has the appearance of a tiny bonfire, with bright miniature flames leaping up from its woody base; is it too late to rename it the fire fungus?

I reach the southern edge. Through a break in the edge trees, the Dower House is visible in the distance, washed in late afternoon autumn sunshine. Only in autumn, in late afternoon, shortly before sunset, do you get that golden orange light, which is now setting light to the stone and brick of the ruin. Lost in thought and on meandering route, I stumble upon a further veteran, or maybe ancient oak, and I wonder that I have not properly regarded this giant before. Its fissured, robust girth is striking, rising up to a rambling crown and sometimes truncated branches, giving this old one a haphazard battle-scarred appearance. One of its massive fallen limbs lies prone on the ground in a tangle of bramble and honeysuckle. A shiny-cased beetle scuttles hurriedly over scarred, bleached wood on the fallen branch as I stoop for closer inspection.

This oak stands on the very edge of the wood, hard against the stock fence to the parkland. Its northern, eastern and western flanks are largely accessible, but its southern face is crowded by clinging bramble and the sinewy tendrils of the weaving honeysuckle. I must hurry if I am not to lose the light of the day.

I begin at the western face, using the fallen limb to gain

better access. I make steady, measured progress to the south-eastern quarter where I do careful sorties with thorns and cord. Eventually, I establish a girth at around shoulder height of 554 centimetres, making this oak the largest girthed tree in the wood. But is it the oldest, given the wood edge location, where there is better access to light? I estimate, very roughly, given the location, southern aspect and protection from the worst of the prevailing winds, an age of around four hundred years. So, whilst being the largest of the old ones, and having an ancient appearance, it does not take the crown.

I make my way back to the far side of the wood and back to the wooden footbridge, following paths heading generally north and east. The journey home produces no more candidates older than those we have recorded. And so, it turns out that the first veteran we measured in the south-western corner of the wood, outcompeting the surrounding sycamore and sweet chestnut, with a potential age of around 550 years, is the oldest of the old. And long may it stand.

An accidental consequence of today's visit is that, along with general enjoyment of the wood and its confines, I have made friends today: individual veteran trees that will stay in memory and that will remain familiar to me on my wanderings long after this journal is complete.

FORTY-EIGHT

OF THE BIRCH

Saturday, 12 October 2019 – 16.35

I am due to pick up the youngest daughter from her shift at the hotel later, so I decide to park up at the Fawsley side of the parkland. The persistent rain of the morning has blown over, leaving ragged grey cloud. The wood awaits out of view beyond the northern horizon in front of me.

I make my way up the steady grassy slope. To my left, a little way off, a cedar of Lebanon stands in isolation, magnificent in the landscape. Its dark boughs splay in terraces, casting shade, tapering gradually upwards; it is exotic and the language of parkland. To my right, in the distance, a black sheep stands out from the flock, head down but oblivious. Cheeky jackdaws ride playfully on the edge of the wind high above the parkland treetops.

About halfway up the slope, I pass a barefoot walker and

his booted companion, and we exchange 'hellos' as if walking in the autumn countryside, wellies in hand, is the most natural thing in the world to do. I maintain eye contact and wonder at how he manages to avoid ambush thistles. Perhaps he does this all the time, walking barefoot, rooted in nature, and it is me that is missing out. As I reach the top of the slope, in amongst the parkland beeches are numerous parasol fungi forming their own miniature parkland, some capped as big as dinner plates. They serve to remind me that I can put it off no longer – the next entry has to concern fungi.

I enter the wood at the beginning or end of the avenue and drop down the muddy narrow path. After sharing with a friend my growing collection of fungi photographs, he has set me a challenge today, and that is for me to find slime mould within the wood; so, I am on the hunt again, eyes peeled. I spot a solitary dome-capped fungus, white in colour, little more than five millimetres in all dimensions, at shoulder height, nestled in the mossy fork of an old, gnarly elder. Although delightful, and probably the smallest fungus I am likely to see this season, it is not what I am looking for.

I turn right a short way into the wood, heading east along the path skirting the southern edge. All around me, in the canopies and the understorey, and across the woodland floor, vibrant greens are slowly transitioning to browns, yellows and golds. The pathway continues to fill with the fallen leaves of the sycamore and sweet chestnut. I am heading in the direction of the firs where there may be a better opportunity to spot slime mould on the myriad fallen logs and mouldering stumps.

I pass the three birches, as if to remind me that I really ought to tell you something of the birch now. The birch (*Betula pendula*) is a fast-growing deciduous tree, which in uncrowded conditions can reach heights of up to twenty-six metres, but it is relatively short-lived. The crown is triangular shaped, and later on in its life, the boughs take on a weeping appearance. The birch's most distinctive feature is its bark – it is unmistakeable and gives the tree its name; the bark is silver in colour, smooth on young trees and often producing papery strips. The silver bark in older trees becomes fissured and scarred. The leaves are ovate/triangular in shape and around seven centimetres long with sawtoothed edges. The leaves turn golden-yellow in the autumn. The male catkins appear in early winter and are brownish in colour. In the spring, the male catkins distend and turn yellow. The female catkins are not so long and are green in colour. The tiny seeds, of which the tree produces many thousands, have papery wings either side of the tiny seed pods. Their winged, small size enables the seeds to be distributed widely by the winds. I can personally attest to this; there is a mature silver birch a couple of doors away at home; in the late summer, our bathroom and laundry floor are littered with the windblown seeds, which have an uncanny knack of entering the house seemingly even when windows and doors are shut.

I know from previous research that the birch is versatile and has numerous bushcraft uses. The birch can be tapped in early spring, when the sap is rising (when the leaves of the hazel first break bud), for its sweet, clear liquid. The drilled hole must be sufficiently plugged as a barrier to disease. The bark of the birch can be 'cooked' in airtight conditions to produce birch bark tar, which, amongst other uses, can be used for joint sealing. The bark can also be used for making containers, but finding sufficient quantities of bark unspoilt by fissures is a challenge.

I leave the row of silver birch behind, the oval leaves just showing the first signs of autumn, and continue heading east. I pass the Great Beech and head into the fir grove. Whilst there are fungi to be seen nearly wherever you look in the wood at the moment, it is almost impossible to tread anywhere within the confines of the firs without stepping on the delicate fruiting bodies. They carpet the woodland floor in singles and in clusters and adorn stumps and fallen trunks. I make my way slowly, inspecting logs and decaying timber for possible slime mould, and whilst I spot potential candidates – including grey gelatinous masses and whole stumps speckled in bright white and yellows – I think they are fungal fruiting bodies and therefore technically not slime moulds.

I am losing the light due to a combination of both the lowering sun and passing cloud and make my way slowly back (although still on the hunt), heading due west. Before I reach the western edge of the grove, I spot in the low light what I initially perceive to be a strange-looking fungus growing out of the side of a weather-stained trunk, but it turns out to be a slug – a wood slug. He, or she, is on the side of the trunk at about a height of two or so feet above the ground and is making its way slowly over the damp, rough bark of the fir. On my return home, and in consulting the field guide, it turns out I was not far away with my initial naming; it is actually a tree slug, pale in colour, with distinct frill or 'foot fringe' as it is properly known. The tentacles on the head of the slug are darker in colour compared to the body. The tree slug is at home in the wood and feeds on algae growing on ancient trunks. It is also quite photogenic and a first for me within the confines of the wood.

As I make my way back to the exit, I disturb a solitary roe deer. She bounds away to my right, white rump bouncing. She stops though, stock still, about forty or so yards away and glances back over her flank. Satisfied that I do not intend to pursue, she moves casually on, without urgency, and is soon lost to the trunks and tangles. Just before my exit, and with time running short, I spot a half-decent chestnut in the leaf litter. The harvest may be alright after all.

As I emerge back into the landscape of veteran beeches and parasol fungi, the setting sun sits just above the near horizon to my right, casting golden light and long shadow. He keeps me company for a time as I make my back down the long, steady slope to the car.

FORTY-NINE
OF DECAY

Sunday, 20 October – 14.15

I park up close to the church and swap trainers for boots. High overhead, above the village, buzzards call to each other; there are six in total: a family of four and a transient pair. They wheel in engaging graceful spirals over the landscape, inquisitive of each other, before going their separate ways, our family out over their woodland home and the transient pair due west, perhaps in search of territory. I share the moment with a gardener taking a short break from tending the borders to the front of her neat little cottage. My craned neck and gaze up into the sky has caught her attention and she too looks up. I comment on how nice this spot is, in the shadow of the church and spreading horse chestnut on the neat Church Green. The gardener declares that she is local – 'born and bred'. The church bells ring quarter past the hour.

I drop down the narrow path, its width restricted by a top-heavy privet hedge enclosing the garden beyond. On my right, I spot a distinctive game trail, very obvious up the steep bank of the sunken path. A bare earthen track runs up and under the hedge, and on closer inspection, I spot the impression of a single partial badger print, pads and claws distinctly visible. The young Nene babbles away audibly in the culvert beneath my feet at the base of the valley. I head up the opposite slope and into the pasture while the buzzards continue to 'mew' their sombre calls overhead, and distant human voices can be heard beyond the hedgerow to my right.

At the far edge of the pasture, I clamber up and over the leaning fence and onto the slick surface of the footbridge and into the confines of the wood. I drop down to the confluence of the streams and jump over their swollen flow. The wood is busy, well, relatively so, and I decide to head off path due west, making my way slowly, avoiding sporadic falling sweet chestnuts which 'thud' to the leaf-strewn ground. All-round me, growing from mouldering stumps or mossy trunks or simply from the leaf litter, are fungi of all different shapes, sizes and colours. There has been an explosion of these fruiting bodies, and it is nearly impossible to walk without destroying their delicate structures. So, it is appropriate and not before time that I tell you something of decay and fungi now. Probably best that you make that cuppa and settle down; you are in for a long entry.

I have spent the last few months recording and photographing my wood fungi discoveries and have painstakingly sought to identify each one. I have recorded around fifty different species, and there are a few more that I simply have not been able to give a name to. Even armed with a vast number of online sources of information and the two guidebooks from my own library, I have found identification a significant challenge, involving both time and patience. You see, the one thing I have discovered through my own observations and research (and please tell me if I am wrong) is that fungal fruiting bodies or mushrooms or toadstools – whatever your preference is – change their appearance through their relatively short lifespan, and it seems to me that there is subtle variation in form and colouring within the same species (although that view is reached on the basis of comparison of my own observations and photographs with the vast library of information out there) and strong visual similarity between different species, making identification very difficult and fraught with the potential for a high degree of error, especially to my untrained eye. And it is precisely for these reasons that I make no attempt to advise on whether the fungi I have found and identified are edible or not; I will leave it to you to do your own research and to make your own decision about consumption. I would never pick or eat fungi without an expert present, and I am no expert. There is simply too much potential for accidental poisoning. As a friend once said to me 'remember, you only eat the wrong one once'.

It is clear, just from my observations, that fungi must make up a significant part of the biomass and biodiversity of the wood – after all, the number of fungi I have recorded (and there will be more) must be equal to or more than the other species present in the wood, apart from maybe the insects.

Although it might be tempting to think of fungi as plants, they do not have the ability as plants do to convert sunlight into food and energy and instead derive food from living or dead organisms. And in 'feeding' on dead organisms, fungi assist in the breaking down of the organic matter of the wood, releasing nutrients back into the environment, which can then be recycled by other organisms such as plants and trees. In this way, fungi play a very important role in the continuity of the wood. If fungi did not exist and perform this essential function, there would be no decomposition of material and no recycling of nutrients back into the cycle of life.

On my last visit, I stumbled across a decomposing conifer trunk in one of the dense fir groves in the wood and was fascinated; the trunk had obviously been reasonably substantial in its lifetime, and the ghost of its former shape and extent was evident on the undisturbed ground in the form of a brown stain of fibrous decayed woody material. And all that remained was the harder, more resilient and as yet undecomposed harder heartwood of the tree. But I assume this too will rot away in time. This tree's loss will be another's gain; the nearby firs will be directly benefitting from the nutrients and elements slowly leaching back into the ground around their network of roots.

Fungi are remarkable organisms; when you walk through your wood, as I do through mine, over the woodland floor, you are walking over a microscopic network of many thousands of metres, or even miles of filaments known as hyphae which, when connected together, form mycelium. You may have seen mycelium present as fine white threads when inspecting the underside of bark on a dead tree or perhaps even in the disturbed ground.

The fruiting bodies of the fungi, also known as mushrooms, or even toadstools, are formed from hyphae tissue. The mushrooms, or sporocarp, if you want to give them their official name, produce spores from pores and gills on the underside of caps and brackets. If you come across a bracket fungus, and there appears to be a brown, stained area beneath the fungi, this is most likely staining caused by the release of spores. And if you ever agitate a puff ball (as I am sure most of us will have done), the greeny black cloud that is energetically ejected is also spores. The released spores are windblown and eventually settle, and in the right conditions, they will germinate to form new hyphae and continue the cycle.

Wohlleben, in his book: *The Hidden Life of Trees*, describes how the extensive network of mycelium below our feet is used by trees to convey information between themselves, and even between competitors, about such matters as insect attack, water depletion and other threats. The recently coined term for this is: the 'Wood Wide Web'. But in the same way that fungi can help trees in a symbiotic way, certain types of fungi, such as honey fungus, spell the death knell for trees, essentially attacking the tree and breaking down cell structure while it is still alive.

Today we will mention and describe, and attempt to identify, around twenty different types of fungi. I should mention that the media describes this year as being a particularly good year for fungi, so it appears that we have been lucky.

I continue off path, heading steadily west.

I pass coffee– and cream-coloured mushrooms; the caps are around five to seven centimetres across, with a cream-coloured outer edge darkening to coffee, before finishing in a darker coloured 'nipple' in the centre. The centre of some caps are darker than others. The underside is creamy in colour and formed in gills which are designed to disperse the spores. I think this is the fruiting body of the mealy funnel fungus (*Clitocybe vibecina*) which can be found in proliferation in the wood at present.

A little further on and in amongst a tangle of fallen branches and this year's leaves, I spot three toadstools growing tall on slender stalks topped by a conical cap. The stalks are grey in colour and the cap is light at the edge, darkening to a light grey. The tall, slender grey stalks are this fungus's most distinctive feature. I think it is the snapping bonnet (*Mycena vitilis*), which must take its name from the 'bonnet'-shaped cap.

Nearby, to my right, growing out from the mossy side of a fallen trunk, is a cluster of seemingly white fungi, contrasting sharply with the green, mossy background. On closer inspection, the short stalks of the fungus are cream-coloured and the cap – around two to three centimetres in diameter – is cream, conical in shape, darkening slightly to the centre but still overall light in colour. On my knees and looking up at the gills, they are alternate lighter and darker in colour. I think this fungus is the common bonnet (*Mycena galericulata*).

I continue on, briefly joining one of the defined paths, and come across a recently fallen oak; its lesser branches lay ruined and scattered, the leaves wilted and sad-looking. I walk the length of the trunk and nearly miss a tiny orange mushroom, comprising a delicate filament-like stalk and domed cap, bright orange in colour. The mushroom is no more than five millimetres in height and the conical dome is no more than two to three millimetres in diameter. I think this delicate, tiny, perfect fungus is the orange bonnet (*Mycena acicula*).

I spot more common bonnet, growing from mossy trunk and branch. And at the base of another trunk, there is a cluster of fungi, growing out of the decaying wood, around forty in number, and whilst all of the same species, they vary slightly in size. The fungi are light in colour, darkening slightly to the conical centre and the stalks are the same colour as the cap. I think this cluster of fungi is angel's bonnet (*Mycena arcangeliana*). I leave this perfect photogenic cluster of mushrooms behind and continue wandering, eventually into the new, or not so new, plantation – there are more fungi to be seen of the same species we have already mentioned.

Beside the path is a tree stump, trunkless and upturned, upon which sits, limpet-like, a lone ladybird, bright red with eighteen black spots and white cheeks. After some online research, having exhausted my various guides, I think this particular ladybird is the harlequin ladybird (*Harmonia axyridis*). I had no idea there are so many types of ladybird! I am distracted from the observation of the ladybird by a squirrel bolting stealthily through the undergrowth not far away, looking for safe refuge, followed in hot pursuit, crashing noisily over the woodland floor, by an eager dog. I watch as the squirrel finds refuge and the dog carries on, oblivious. I am reminded of Ollie and his antics for a time.

I continue heading west and spot a curious sight; in an old scar at the base of a mature sycamore, there is a fairy house, with mossy entrance door, pencil-drawn window and tiny signpost announcing: 'We are fairies. We live here' – as if there could be any doubt. It is Fairy House No. 6, by the way, on account of the No.6 written below the window. I wonder where the other five fairy houses are? I leave the no doubt watchful and tricksy fairies in peace, cross the main track with the archway glimpsed to my left and head into the eastern half of the wood, where the going off path is a little easier.

I have meant to mention for a while that for me, the eastern side of the wood, to the east of the main track, generally has a different feel to the western side. I think it is simply down to perhaps that the eastern half has less ground cover, and maybe slightly lower tree density, and more plantation than natural growth. A subtle change in the character and atmosphere is the result. But that could of course all be nonsense.

Anyway, I make my way up the rising ground and into the eastern half proper. I have not gone very far before I spot more fungi to describe. There is a trunk, of which tree I am not sure. It is branchless and is leaning out at an acute angle, propped aloft only by the coppiced multiple stems of an adjacent hazel. Arranged along the length of the trunk are fifteen or so bracket fungi. They are white-edged but with a rusty red topside darkening to the centre. The rust-coloured upper side is flat, but the white underside is angled. And the bright white underside is heavily pockmarked by noticeable deep pores, some round, some elongated. So heavily pockmarked is the underside, and arranged in such a pattern, that I am reminded of the pierced fan corals in our seas. I think this particular bracket fungus is blushing bracket (*Daedaleopsis confragosa*). The blushing bracket has a cap of between three to fifteen centimetres wide, is sharp-edged, and when the underside is scratched, the flesh bruises pink, hence the name. I leave the blushing bracket behind (I have since attempted to find the same leaning trunk and fungi but without success) and continue on up the steadily rising ground, past partial fairy rings and long-abandoned warrens.

After a while, I come across a hollow – a noticeable depression in the woodland floor; it is damp and criss-crossed by broken branches. I recognise this hollow immediately – it has been a long time since I was last here, probably not since I was a child, and in mainly sticking to the well-walked paths, there is no reason why I would have come across it over the intervening years. Dad used to bring us to this spot though, off path, and I have been looking for it for a long time. For no other reason than to confirm it is a memory from this wood. For a while, I had begun to suspect that it was not, and I was getting confused with somewhere else. But here it is, unremarkable, but it is still a comforting rediscovery.

Nearby, I spot two of our smaller fungi. The first you know, but since it has become my favourite, I will describe it again; it is the yellow stagshorn fungus (*Calocera viscosa*). In my guidebook, it is named 'yellow antler fungus'. The yellow stagshorn grows to between three to ten centimetres high and can be found on coniferous tree stumps. My example is growing directly from the ground – bright yellow against the backdrop of fallen pine needles and fir cones. I still think it looks like a miniature bonfire. The second are a curiosity; from a heavily decaying log, disintegrating and mossy, are growing numerous black and white erect stalks, little more than a centimetre high. The stalks are black at the base, fading to smoking grey and finally, white tipped. On this particular log, there must be thirty or more of these fungal stalks. After a bit of research and with the help of the previously mentioned photographic guide, I think this curious little fungus is the candlesnuff fungus (*Xylaria hypoxylon*). It does not take much imagination to see how this little fungus got its name.

I continue on, feeling complete and leaving the hollow behind. I wander up towards the high beeches, past the foxglove glade – despite observations much earlier in this journal, I do find a cluster of foxglove rosettes, pensive and ready for spring/summer next year.

Upon entering the lofty high beeches, I spot a fallen branch, and from its underside hang – or rather protrude – small fungi, all in a row. They are almost like a mini-bracket, bright porcelain white. And when turned upside down, the fungi are round – to kidney-shaped with radiating close-packed gills. The fungus has very obviously evolved to hang rather than grow upwards like the majority of its relatives. This one does not get mention in my guidebook. I think it is the variable oysterling (*Crepidotus variabilis*). The fruiting body grows attached to the twig or branch by its cap and is between 0.5 to two centimetres in diameter. They are dainty and pretty. Close by is another branch, or rather more like a twig, multi-forked and with dark, shiny bark. Along its length are salmon pink tiny round fungi, the largest being little more than four to five millimetres in diameter. I think it is the coral spot fungus (*Nectria cinnabarina*). Again, the coral spot gets no mention at all in my guide, so I have used the online Amanita photo guide for identification.

As I meander through the high beeches, I am surrounded for a time by two or three nuthatches. Their chorus is joined by Bran croaking from outside of the wood and somewhere in the parkland. I continue on, down to the five-bar gate, up through the conifers, around the Knott and onto the painter's crossroads.

Before we leave the wood today, and this fungal safari, I have two final fungi to describe for you. On top of a large fallen trunk and in amongst more coral spot fungus, I spot black balls in tight, sometimes overlapping, clusters, with an appearance not dissimilar to lumps of coal. This too is absent from my guidebook, but using the Amanita photo guide, I think they are cramp ball fungus (*Daldinia concentrica*). Other names for the cramp ball fungus include 'King Alfred's Cakes' (I do not think explanation is necessary) and 'coal fungus'. The examples I am observing now are between three and seven centimetres across.

And finally for today, and just as I am leaving the wood, I spot another fungus that I have been on the hunt for for a while. It is growing out from a barkless scar of a long-dead oak and appears to have a velvety black texture and is arranged almost like the petals of a flower, around four to five centimetres across. I think it is, rather alarmingly, witches' butter (*Exidia glandulosa*).

As I leave the wood, a jay bids me farewell or, more likely, it is simply saying 'good riddance'. The nearby church clock strikes four.

This is a long entry. I hope I have not bored you but also hope that I have inspired you to look out for your own fungi discoveries in your own wood through the summer and autumn months.

FIFTY

OF SHORTENING DAYS
AND FAIRY RINGS

Sunday, 27 October 2019 – 16.15

The clocks went back overnight, and we march on to the end of the year. It is late Sunday afternoon, bright and clear with a distinct autumnal chill. Em has returned from university for the weekend and keeps me company. The village is Sunday afternoon quiet.

We head in via Brookside Lane, up through the pasture along the muddy and slippery path, following in the footsteps of many other visitors and their canine companions. In the upper pasture, the wood stretches out before us, spreading to our left and right, in all shades of greens and the beginning of subtle autumn hues.

We are greeted by two playful Irish terriers and their staffy side kick. Em breaks stride briefly to give the pack a welcome fuss, and I await her inevitable new puppy question. The pack returns to their owners, and we continue on. Our path crosses a narrow game trail traversing the slope through the short-cropped grass, its route as distinctive as the muddy trail spotted last week. And I wonder again that it must be the badgers.

Within the wood, all is still, and all is quiet.

Just within the edge and beside the path, Em points out a crescent of cream-coloured fungi, and upon closer inspection, it appears that the crescent is actually very nearly a full fairy ring. I enter the ring, not without a degree of trepidation, and pace out its diameter, which roughly equates to an impressive ten metres. Unmolested, but maybe under observation just the same, I leave the circle and rejoin Em on the path. In consulting my field guide on my return home, I identify the fungi as clouded agaric (*Clitocybe nebularis*). The cap has a greyish creamy colour and is either flat or forms a shallow concave funnel and is about handspan in diameter. There are cream-coloured gills on the underside. The fungi are many in number, forming the ring.

We leave the ring behind and wander the paths, passing west of the Knott, skirting its western toe. The wood stands at a tipping point; half of the canopies remain green, while the remainder transition to yellows and oranges. Some trees are more advanced than others; the sweet chestnuts we pass, and sometimes stoop below, are the first to succumb to the shorter days and cold nights, branch and twig adorned with a dressing of golden leaves. More yet lay scattered in our path. While other trees, including the odd chestnut, remain largely in green leaf. A little further on, we pass a beech whose canopy is turning to rich autumn orange.

Em decides that she should like to see the badgers and so we head for the southern sett in the falling light. When we arrive, it is still too light and so we wait and watch a little way off. The leaf-strewn ancient terraces are in sight thirty or so yards in front. Despite our patience and hushed voices, our vigil is in vain and twenty or so minutes later, with the badger family remaining as yet below ground, we must move on if we are to be home in time for dinner. But just as we are set to head off, we halt a moment and stand still while our family of buzzards, all four, fly low over the canopies immediately above our heads, unaware of our presence and deep in conversation.

With the dark encroaching, we follow the western edge to the kissing gate; rather than continue on in the wood and risk the wrath of Mother, we leave its embrace and exit onto the water-logged paddock. The northern edge of the wood to our right tapers to the horizon. Even in the twilight, the autumn colours at the wood edge are evident.

The owl calls farewell as we enter the narrow, sunken path into the valley.

It is full dark by the time we are back at the village greens.

FIFTY-ONE

OF SHADES AND WRAITHS

Thursday, 31 October 2019 – 16.40

It is All Hallows' Eve and close to sundown. Jim and I are heading into the wood via the main track. It is overcast and we both don scarves to ward off the chill. Upon entering the wood, we are greeted by a blackbird 'pinking' away in alarm somewhere amongst the understorey. I take Jim to show her the 'fairy meeting place' I spotted a couple of entries ago at the base of a chestnut. All is quiet, mischief performed elsewhere.

It is a short walk tonight and so we decide on sticking to the main track all the way through the wood. The crows and jackdaws are noisy in the half-light. Their winged silhouettes pass across the silvery gap between the autumn canopies high above our heads.

A trip up the wood at All Hallows' Eve inevitably requires

a ghost story or two. It just so happens that there are two well-known stories of the macabre relating to the wood and park, and I have a couple of my own. The first tale concerns the Dower House. It is hard to imagine, after all, that such a ruin would not have a tale to tell. If you should happen to find yourself near those ruins – out in the park on New Year's Eve, when the last light of the sun dips below the horizon, on a murky winter's day – you may be unlucky enough to have an encounter with the huntsman, dressed in green garb and mounted on his ghostly steed. Eyes bright points of blue fire. Beware, for the huntsman carries a portent of doom for someone close to you.

The next tale is of a crime of passion carried out within the wood itself from a time long past. The tale goes that a wife was returning on foot from a romantic liaison with her lover – perhaps having taken place within the nearby village – and upon her return back through the wood, she was found and confronted by her husband, whereupon, in a fit of rage, her young life was brutally taken. It is said that her spirit forever wanders the woodland paths, lonely and in despair. I have yet to see her.

Jim and I continue on in the twilight before arriving at the five-bar gate. There is a little of the last minutes of light left at the wood edge. The crows and jackdaws continue to call. A light breeze gently stirs the leaves around us. The Dower House remains hidden behind the low, leafy canopies of the oaks. A couple more tales for your now.

When I met the painter at this crossroads last summer, he told me of a time before when he had been painting in the wood late in the day, on the edge of the new plantation, and had witnessed a mysterious hovering globe of light some distance away between the trunks. He paused from his canvas and watched awhile with some trepidation, before the light faded and finally disappeared. He decided it was as good a time as any to finish painting for the day.

My only potential brush with the supernatural was a couple of years ago when walking parallel with the southern edge and in the middle of a perfectly ordinary day. I spotted two figures: two old ladies who were on the path heading in my direction but still some two hundred or so yards distant. The pair were dressed in perfectly normal twenty-first-century clothing appropriate for the day and time of year. I lost sight of them due to the lie of the land between us, but when I had progressed to a point where they should have come back into view, and where they should have been a good deal closer, they were nowhere to be seen. They had disappeared. There were no side paths they could have taken, and I would have seen had they made an about turn or headed off path. I have no explanation as to what could have happened to them, and whilst I was not scared, I was nevertheless perplexed and remain so to this day.

Jim reminds me that her shift at the nearby hotel is fast approaching so we leave the five-bar gate and turn to face the wood interior. We have only been stood facing into the parkland for a short time, but it was enough for the light to retreat and the dark to take its place. By the time we reach the silhouette of the arch, on the edge of full dark, the crows and jackdaws have finally gone to roost.

There is something about moving through the wood at night that means you are never quite at ease, when vague shapes form and dissolve and then reform in the dark, and the most innocent of sounds appear more sinister. To my mind, it is simply an awareness borne out of an ancient primeval instinct to be fearful of the dark and the wood at night and the dangers it would have once held. It is only comparatively recently that we have rationally unlocked the secrets of our woods and forests and in doing so, have dispelled myth and magic. Well, almost.

We leave the wood without incident. No witches or 'bone' fires to be seen.

FIFTY-TWO

OF THE BATS

Sunday, 3 November – 15.45

I am on my way to the footpath, just past the Chapel. A lawnmower breaks the Sunday afternoon silence, rumbling away productively out of sight – it must be the last cut of the year. In the distance ahead of me, a couple, hand in hand, and their faithful dog head off up the lane. The brook is swollen and flows noisily along its course below my feet.

I pass through the kissing gate and out into the field. The grass is cropped short now and the undulations of the ridge and furrow are clearly discernible. I am in the shadow of the trees running along Brookside Lane to my right, but to my left, in an elevated position, the distant hedgerow stands out, striking, illuminated by the late afternoon sun.

On my way up the slippery slope, a solitary crow forages in the short grass; its black head rises and something bright white is grasped in its robust beak. With a deft, subtle and well-practised flick of its head, the white morsel is consumed. Hunger momentarily satisfied, my approach catches his eye, and he pauses his foraging, watchful. I linger briefly and we hold each other's gaze. There is clear intelligence there.

From the upper pasture, the wood is all autumn hues. The last of the day's walkers and wood visitors head in the direction of the village. The crescent moon shines brightly and is vigilant over the wooded horizon.

The wood is peaceful, still and comforting. The light is already falling, but it is still a little way off sunset. I have a choice of three paths and pause, undecided. I have no agenda today. I reach for a coin in my trouser pocket, leaving it to the fates, but there are none. Just my hanky. Ignoring the path either side heading east and west, I strike straight ahead. The fairy ring is still there, a broken white circle amongst the fallen leaves.

The going is very soft underfoot and in places I slip and slide, and in others, I avoid the worst of it. I reach the curiously metalled path and, turning left, heading east on the ancient, cobbled surface, the going is a little easier. As I always do when I tread these smooth, worn stones, I wonder about their age and by whose hand they were laid.

I have not gone very far before a new obstacle lies ruined across my path; an oak, bare of its leaves, long dead, straddles the path. Below the bare trunk, slabs of bark litter the ground, shed violently at the moment of impact. A solitary fungus grows out vertically from the side of the wet trunk; the tree will be a rich source of fungi for years to come. I take the already forming diversion, past the exposed roots of the fallen giant.

I continue on, steadily west, and eventually arrive at the main track. To my right, the track is framed in gold by the autumn beeches; those leaves already fallen lay amongst numerous speckled golds, reds and oranges. I head off path, through the bramble beside the track and up the slope, following roughly the same route as a couple of entries back where I spotted the long-lost hollow. There are still mealy cap and clouded agaric mushrooms to be seen dotted between the pines and the beeches.

I meander and wander between and around trunks and avoiding bracken patches. The wood remains quiet, and even the crows and jackdaws are still tonight. After a while, I find myself at the five-bar gate. It is lighter at the wood edge. The parkland is greens and browns, and the sentinel oaks are on the turn. Even the grass has lost its vibrancy. The same crescent moon hangs bright.

To my surprise, as a substitute for the dragonflies that were absent at this spot this year – at least when I was there – a very late bat flies, on the hunt for equally late insects. A second bat joins the first briefly, two black, leathery silhouettes against the silvery sky. Knowing a little about the habits of bats through my work, it is very late in the year for a bat to be out and about, and I can only think that they must be taking a last opportunity to lay down fat before their hibernation over the long winter, tucked away in some hidden crook or nook within one of the veteran oaks, sheltered from the biting winter wind and harsh frosts.

I reluctantly leave the bats to their winged foraging and make my way back. It is near dark within the confines of the wood and for a while, I lose the path before eventually joining the track running down the long, northern slope of the Knott. As the perfect accompaniment to the stillness and dark, the owl calls out a little way ahead. By reply, further away to the west, perhaps beyond the wood edge, a second owl calls. And to the east, slightly nearer, a third joins the conversation. Their calls fade, albeit by degrees, as I leave the wood and make my way back to the lane.

FIFTY-THREE
OF LAST LIGHT

Friday, 8 November – 16.00

I struggle to capture a perfect moment up the wood in words; good ideas and phrases swarm like noisy bees in my head, but somehow, when you cast them down on the page, they lose their energy and vibrancy and lay taunting.

Anyway, here goes.

I find myself at my favourite spot, late in the day and at the week's end. I lean on the smooth timber – wood behind, parkland in front – and watch the light drain steadily from the day. Another lone walker led the way into the wood, some distance ahead, and is now somewhere abroad in this expanse of trunks. Just him and I and all the wild between.

I listen and hear the wood speak its timeless language. The wind hisses through the last leaves on the beech and sycamore.

The crow cacophony sounds deep within the wood, far off and distant. A single leaf falls, spiralling unseen down to collide softly with the network of branches and twigs before finally coming to rest amongst the patchwork of colours.

More sounds close by: a rustle of leaves but subtlety different and with purpose. A vague deer shape, dark against a darker backdrop, appears at the wood edge nearly within touching distance, unconcerned and unaware. I remain still, breath held and muscles tensed. The deer potters for a short while, head down, without direction, as if looking for something. But then moves slowly away. The moment is fleeting and yet lasts an age.

The silhouetted canopies, less dense now, sway gently against the very last of the day's light.

I make my way back along the kaleidoscope path, colours lost to the dark. Pinpricks of light from a different world beyond flicker between the monolith trunks ahead. The toothed arch emerges from the dark, appearing to hover for a moment, elevated and disorientating, before rooting itself firmly in the present.

FIFTY-FOUR
OF COLOUR

Sunday, 10 November 2019 – 12.45

The title of today's entry could have been about many discoveries and observations – the miniature cascades, new fungi, the deer or the buzzards – but despite all these, today it is about colour, the colour that the edge of winter brings. Those rich veins of gold.

On the wood edge, the ash we spied all the way back in the spring – that ash that told of a dry summer – has shaken off its leaves, without exception, and now stands fully winter bare.

The streams that gather together in the south-western corner of the wood are swollen by the recent poor weather; yesterday brought much rain. The clear water, usually contained within the narrow earthen banks, is washed out over the woodland floor. Miniature waterfalls cascade over miniature terraces formed by fallen logs. The white water froths and bubbles, and all-round is the pervading sound of the water running.

At the southern edge, I make my way along paths with rich, dark surfaces churned by myriad footsteps. The larch, at the base of the deer bank, and amongst the dead bracken, is on the turn: green fading to yellow. I linger and take a step or two off the path, enough to flush out four roe deer, who emerge from the cover of browns and yellows high up on the bank. They traverse the horizon in leaps and bounds against the backdrop of magnificent beech and the blue sky beyond. Further on, and three more roe deer follow in their path, eventually becoming at one with the wood.

I pass our three birches; not two weeks ago, the trees were in full leaf, albeit on the turn, but now, just like the ash, the leaves lay about the trunks in a dense, yellow mat, and for now the birches rest, awaiting the return of spring.

By design and intention, I divert off the southern path and make my way up the slope to the Great Beech. The fallen giant and its sister are a gateway to the stand of beech and to a world of autumn colour. All is gold, accentuated by the sun shining through the wood edge, illuminating each leaf in vibrant colour. From base to crown, the trees shine, radiant. I move through the spectacle silently and pleasantly aghast. Other walkers have come to enjoy the scene, which is as dramatic and startling as the carpet of blue we witnessed at the beginning of spring. In this wood at least, no other tree can hold a candle to the beech in its autumn finery. But even now, while the beech waits for colder weather to shake off its coat of colour, or perhaps not, brown buds, sharp and pointy, already enclose next spring's leaves.

I dawdle, slowing my pace, selfishly wanting this space to

myself. When the other walkers have moved sufficiently far ahead and behind, I continue on but with reluctance.

Where the beeches begin to mix with the firs, I spot something I had hoped to bring you news of but had all but given up hope of mention. It is another fungus and, whilst predated on by the deer, and consequently looking dishevelled and incomplete, it is unmistakably the most 'toadstool'-looking of all our native fungi – it is of course the fly agaric (*Amanita muscaria*) with bright red glossy cap, dotted with white spots. This find is a nice rounding off of my fungi hunt this year. I really did not think it would get mention. I leave the beech and the battered fly agaric behind and continue my full circuit of the wood.

The remainder of the walk is mostly uneventful; I see now familiar fungi, the odd industrious squirrel and a glimpse of our buzzards rising on the thermals, visible through a break in the canopy in the northern part of the wood.

The highlight of today though is autumn colour, a final gift as we teeter on the edge of winter.

FIFTY-FIVE

OF LICHEN

Saturday, 16 November – 15.15

Either side of the wooden footbridge grow two larch trees; I had not noticed them before, lost, or at least merging with the other green canopies. But now, as the leaves fall and canopies thin, and the needles of the larch fade to yellow, they form the perfect gateway to the Autumn Wood.

As I draw near the bridge and larches, a buzzard takes flight from the wood edge just to my left – large, rounded wings carry the mottled brown raptor gracefully over the close-cropped pasture to a solitary oak, just beyond the far hedgerow behind me. I turn and follow its course. Before the buzzard has fully settled, its flight and arrival in the oak has attracted the unwanted attention of two crows. The crows swoop in and land on the branch above the buzzard's perch, close, but not too close. Enough, though, for the buzzard to know that while the crows remain watchful and devious, it will have no peace, so it takes flight and moves on.

High above us, that is the crows and I, jackdaws return to the wood and parkland from a day spent foraging out in the country somewhere. They come in squadrons, and I watch them pass, more than forty or fifty in number.

Within the wood, the canopies are thinning; views from the path are less confined, opening out, and the wood all-round is all the more lighter for the lost leaves that now carpet the woodland floor and its network of paths and rides. I do a half circuit today, up and over the Knott and along the southern and western edges. There is no wind – not a breath; not a sound. I am struck by the silence of the wood. It is deafening, as they say. There is no distant murmur of voices and no backdrop soundscape of twenty-first-century noise. The silence reinforces the solitude and sense of timelessness. I like the wood best at such times.

I am on the hunt again today. There is a miniature world within the wood that remains largely unseen and easily overlooked, but it is everywhere: above you, beside you, speckling trunks and in dense matts on high branches. It comes in different colours and forms, and it is neither plant nor animal. It is lichen, and if you are wondering about pronunciation, in Britain it is pronounced 'lich-in' with a distinct 'chu' sound in the middle, whereas our American friends might pronounce it as 'lyken' with the 'i' sounding like a 'y'.

Lichen is actually two organisms comprising of fungi and algae living together in a symbiotic relationship; the fungi, unable to synthesise sunlight to produce sugar, rely on the algae to do this, and the algae benefit from the physical structure provided by the fungus, known as the thallus, providing optimum living conditions for the algae. This is, however, a very simple explanation of the relationship which I suspect may be far more complicated.

In my wanderings today, I think I have spotted nine different species of lichen, but I have found that identification is even more of a challenge than fungi and that was hard, so I apologise for inevitable error. I have identified my lichen by sight only, using the photographs within the helpful guide to name the different types and by choosing those that the author has already recorded in our part of the UK and which are more common.

The following is the name and brief description of the lichens I have spotted on today's trip.

The first I spot is growing on the upside of a wrist-thick branch just above head height. It has the appearance of a pale, almost dusty, green, straggly plant about seven millimetres in all directions. Each branch, which are actually known as 'thallus', is wiry and around three millimetres in width and seven millimetres long. I think this is *Ramalina farinacea* which is one of the commonest of the Ramalina species, found on the bark of trees throughout Great Britain.

The next lichen is growing in dense flat mats over a branch on the same tree. It is grey-green in appearance (alien and a little unwholesome), with lobes that vary between being flat, curved or even with a concave surface and then crinkly at the edges. I think this is *Hypogymnia physodes* which is also common on trees and distributed throughout Great Britain.

I have my eye in now and continue moving on path below the canopies. There is not a tree or branch that is not adorned to a lesser or greater extent by the greys, green and yellows.

I spot an oak, semi-mature and solid and reliable. Its

northern flank is a patchwork of dark bark, lush green moss and pale green lichen, which coats this side of the tree to above head height in a nearly unbroken, tactile, grainy mat. There are two potential contenders for this species of lichen; it might be *Lepraria incana* which is common on trees and other media in eastern Britain, according to the guide. But honestly, it could equally be *Fellhanera viridisorediata*, which is of a brighter green but also common on trees.

I continue on, on constant lookout for new specimens, although in truth, they are everywhere.

I spot a sycamore, not particularly old, and amongst the greens and browns there are bright, almost white, roughly formed disks with a granular surface. On closer inspection, the disks are very light green, lightening to almost white (with a hint of pink?) at the margins. Despite extensive searching in the guidebook and online, this one has me stumped – I initially thought that it might be *Haematomma ochroleucum*, but that species only grows exceptionally on trees. I will keep researching.

The next and final lichen I spot is visible as a yellow-green stain on the trunk on an old oak – it could either be *Chrysothrix candelaris*, which is common on oak, or *Chrysothrix flavovirens*, which is common on older trees.

I am sure there are many more to spot, with subtle variations in colour and form, but I think you need an expert present if you want to name them.

FIFTY-SIX

OF THE NIGHT WOOD

Thursday, 21 November 2019 – 20.20

No Moon. No stars. Just the enfolding dark. The night sky is heavy and low, tinted subtle orange. It shrouds the tops of the dark mass of hills to the north. Spots of rain are windblown to smack gently against exposed faces.

We follow the hard path, and ahead of us, the wood is a formless dark band caught between ground and sky.

Past the arch, in our circle of artificial light, the pocket of wood is greys and silver shades. Trunks form into view, grey monoliths whose crowns remain hidden, before fading away behind, consumed by the dark. Beyond our protective pool of light, just sufficient to hold the probing dark at bay, the wood and wild lies hidden. Watchful.

Beasts crash in surprise away from our intrusion and grey wings clatter in the treetops. On the woodland floor, in tangles and in thickets, snouts and muzzles and twitching noses pause, beady eyes marking our passing and the unwelcome intrusion into their night-time world.

Where the winding path narrows, choked by clutching bramble, single file passage becomes necessary, and our alien bodies cast giant shambling shadows over the curtain of trunks ahead.

The weather is a steady drizzle as we leave the wood and its creatures to their night-time solace.

FIFTY-SEVEN
OF BIRDS

Sunday, 24 November 2019 – 14.30

As I negotiate the kissing gate and follow the muddy path into the ridge and furrow, I am greeted by a scruffy, grey-muzzled terrier standing guard, silent. His name is 'Teddy', apparently, and he is currently ignoring Mother, who beckons him from up the grassy slope to my left. Mother sounds increasingly impatient while a stubborn 'Teddy' warily marks my passing.

From the upper pasture, the wood edge is yellow hazel below and brown-leaved oak above. The drizzle is heavy enough to form a mist within which the constant canopy ahead fades to lighter and lighter greys. The wooded horizon is fully lost to the murk.

Within the wood, I turn right, heading east, following the northern edge. I pass rich green holly, prominent now that the deciduous trees wear their autumn colours or no colours at all. The odd holly sprig is still in berry, and I wonder if they might be there in a couple of weeks' time. The streams are still swollen, and the marsh is now a standing pool of water. Our marsh plants which stubbornly refused to flower during the summer are bent, forlorn and in disarray. I have my wellies on and decide to cross the shallow pool with the assistance of a submerged log and the bare, spindly canopy of a young hazel. Despite the support, one booted foot enters the murk and soft pool bed, sinking and releasing foul gasses of decaying organic matter.

A little way past the marsh are the gateway larches. I leave the wood briefly via the slick footbridge to inspect their autumn progress. The needles are now fully yellow, at least those few that remain – the majority, especially those from the lower branches, lay spent among the other colours of the woodland floor.

Back within the wood, I pass a mature multi-stemmed sweet chestnut. Its skeletal branches glisten with the weather. The way south steadily rises and soon I am in an autumn woodscape of dark trunks, bare canopies, leaf-strewn ground and mist, which limits views and softens vistas. Of all the times I have been up the wood since the beginning of September, today's visit feels the most autumnal. A wood in preparation and readiness for the dark and cold of the winter months ahead. Even the profusion of fungi we observed a short while ago are mainly gone.

In the rhododendron glade, the skies are empty and still. The previously head-high, vibrant green bracken is now wet, brown and little more than shin height. Our young oak tree is now visible with the retreat of the bracken, standing in isolation, its branches bare but its twigs already buddied. The four marble galls still adorn the tree, stained dark. Just beyond the glade, I branch off path, up the slope in the direction of the lofty southern edge. I pass a solitary young beech, chest height, still in green leaf, taking the opportunity to make the very most of the last light of the year, while its elders, high above, shake off the last of the year's leaves.

I continue heading east.

Our larch, at the base of the deer bank on the southern edge, is now a splash of colour dressed in yellows and gold, in pleasant contrast to the drab brown surroundings – the canopies of the mature beech behind are mainly bare. The larch will be the same before too long.

The sister to the Great Beech is also now completely bare – not a single leaf remains. I wonder if the bees are now settled and warm, ready for winter? Within the ragged, hollow stump of the Great Beech, in amongst the ferns and the discarded beech and oak leaves, I spy six puff balls – perfect spheres and dirty white. At top centre of each ball there is a small opening, earthy green in colour and access to countless thousands of spores.

I make my way down through the beeches, the same beeches that only a couple of entries back were startling in autumn colour. Now their leaves carpet the ground in an unbroken golden-brown cover. Skirting close to the wood edge here, I disturb a roosting pheasant; he bursts energetically from the canopies just to my right and out into the parkland, calling harshly as he goes. I watch his less than graceful glide, long tail twitching, down and into the bracken some way off.

I know that we are a long way into this entry, and I have made no mention of its title 'Of the Birds', but the wood has been quiet today, just the odd distant call of a woodpecker and jackdaw, and so I thought that I would be without inspiration and leave mention of the birds until another, more appropriate, time. But, as I head down the main track away from the southern edge and parkland, I am surrounded for a time by a large flock of long-tailed tits, maybe as many as ten in number – it is hard to tell. They are scattered in the hazels beside the path, moving from branch to branch and twig to twig on the hunt, alighting briefly before moving on, in constant chatter as they go. They are little balls of soft feather and greys, whites and blacks in colour, with tiny eyes and beak and distinctive long tail.

With inspiration renewed, let me tell you something of the wood's birds now.

This journey has been as much about the birds, as it has the trees and plants and other beasts of the wood. We have listened to and observed the territorial red-breasted robin and disturbed blackbirds in thickets – heard but not seen. We have watched the cheeky jackdaws gathering their train in their tens and twenties and admired Bran and his partner courting in the winds. The buzzards have soared in spirals far above our heads and we have been in the constant company of the ever-present tits. We have been startled by the abrasive alarm of the jay and left melancholy by the soulful hoot of the owl. And not forgetting the frenetic energy of the nuthatch. But you read so much now about the decline in bird populations, and, despite my observations, I wonder how healthy the bird numbers in our wood are.

It turns out that I am not the first to have observed and enjoyed the birds of our particular wood. A little while ago, in discussing the wood and its birds with an acquaintance, he mentioned a book about woodland birds by Eric Simms and subsequently lent me his well-kept copy, aptly named *Woodland Birds*. In turns out that our wood gets several mentions, and clearly Mr Simms spent a good deal of time here in the 1940s and '50s and later. In particular, Mr Simms undertook a survey of the breeding bird population in the wood between 1946 and 1950 – we can use his results as a comparison of my own unscientific casual observations around seventy years later. But, before I do, Mr Simms provides a brief description of the wood back at that time, observing that they wood comprised predominantly pedunculate oak supplemented by scots pine, larch, beech and ash. He further observed that the wood had a scrub layer of occasional hazel, sweet chestnut and holly and extensive bramble and honeysuckle ground cover.

There have been some changes. The wood continues to have a healthy population of pedunculate oak, but in certain parts, beech is the dominant tree species (north and north-eastern) and ash is almost entirely absent save for a few specimens on the northern edge of the wood. Hazel is proliferative in the wood now, especially at its edges, and could not be described as occasional, and nor could the sweet chestnut or holly which have clearly grown in number and maturity since 1949. By far the biggest change is the presence of sycamore, now proliferative in the wood and presumably invasive.

It is interesting to note that bramble has not lost its hold on the woodland floor, but there appears to be considerably less honeysuckle now and the absence of mention of bracken and fern by Mr Simms is telling – I wonder if the success of the bracken is at the expense of the honeysuckle?

A further noticeable change in the intervening years is the planting of Scots pine, spruce and firs for commercial timber production. Mr Simms himself observes, on what must have been a return visit many years later, that through felling and planting of conifers larger areas of the wood have changed considerably since his 1949 visit. Despite the changes, I am sure that, at least for me, the wood remains just as enchanting today as it was back in 1949.

Back to the birds.

Mr Simms' book sets out the results of a survey he undertook of breeding bird pairs from 1946 to 1950 – using the table and comparing the results against my own observations, there are, I think, notable changes from Mr Simms' time to today.

There is no mention of ravens in Mr Simms' list of breeding pairs at all, whereas I am convinced that there is at least one breeding pair resident in and around the wood. There is also no mention of buzzards and again I am certain that the wood has at least one breeding pair who successfully raised two chicks this year – that family we have observed on many occasions. The buzzards are now a common site throughout the Midland's countryside.

Another omission is the tawny owl. I have observed, or at least heard, three male tawny owls with territories in and around the wood and at least one female (although I have recently learned that male tawny owls also produce the 'keewick' contact call).

Other winners include the jays, jackdaws and common crows which I think have all seen significant increases in population since Mr Simms' survey. And of course, not forgetting the woodpeckers – I have personally witnessed a marked increase in their numbers over my time of visiting the wood.

There are notable losers however, compared to Mr Simms' survey, whose populations appear to have significantly declined and in some instances are now entirely absent (although I am no expert at bird calls!) – these include the wren (although there are still a few pairs), chaffinch (I recall seeing just one in the last five years), tree creeper, willow warbler, cuckoo and starling. The cuckoo appears to be a very infrequent visitor, and I do not ever recall seeing a single starling within the wood confines.

On a more positive note, there are species whose populations I suspect remain reasonably static and are still present in the wood in considerable numbers – these include the tits (great, coal, blue and long-tailed – ever-present) and robins and blackbirds.

It is apparent by way of rounding up that it is the larger bird species who are the winners, at the expense of our smaller native bird species.

The long-tailed tits move on, mesmerisingly, through the intertwined canopies, their contact calls fading gradually into the distance.

I meander back along leaf-strewn paths below skeletal trees to my exit.

One last note today – as if by farewell, the female tawny owl utters her 'keewick' call, and a long way off, beyond this patch of perfect woodland, a lone male answers her call.

FIFTY-EIGHT
OF THE WHITE

Saturday, 30 November 2019 – 07.20

The previous entry was meant to be the last one of autumn, but the weather forecast promised a brief arctic blast for today. And wanting to include at least one record of the first frosts before we finish this journal, I have squeezed in one last autumn visit.

It is early now and before sunrise. I am in a world of white; each blade of grass, each twig and bud and coronet seed head are adorned in a rime of white, frigid crystals. This white landscape is enfolded in a shroud of unbroken blanketing fog. A monochrome world.

From the upper pasture, the wood is a vague, formless mass in the vista of white. Only when I am nearly upon them do the frosted, leafless canopies at the wood edge reveal themselves twig by branch from the shroud. A distant owl hoots farewell to the night, and a closer cockerel heralds the day.

Within the wood and the protection of tree cover, the probing frost has been kept at bay, but the fog is stealthy, seeping between and around trunks. I wander the muddy, slippery pathways alone. The frost has not spared the rhododendron glade; green bramble leaves, brown fern fronds and brown and gold leaves of all different shapes and sizes cast over the glade floor are edged in crystalline silver. This white world within the wood is fully encircled by dark branch and trunk. The last leaves fall, succumbing to the biting wrench of the cold. The squirrels chatter quarrelsomely in the treetops and a muntjac or roe barks far off in the acres of wood.

I emerge from the embrace of the wood back into the white to the sound of the church bells striking half past the hour. I need not turn and look back to know that by degrees the blanketing fog swallows the wood behind me.

That is the end of our journey through the Autumn Wood. Let us now re-enter the Winter Wood with adolescent hopes of deep snow.

PART FIVE

RETURN TO WINTER WOOD

FIFTY-NINE

OF THE SQUIRREL

Sunday, 1 December 2019 – 14.30

It is the first day of December and the first day of winter. It is chilly but not the frigid white world it was yesterday. A robin with its festive redbreast leads the way in short, looping flights down into the valley, along the sunken path, its ceiling now mostly bare. I pass by holly in rich red berry. Out in the pasture, I am in cold shade, but away to my left, beyond the hedgerow, the treetops of the wood on the rising ground are illuminated gold by the low sun.

I enter the wood and carry on straight, over the streams and in the direction of the Knott. On its long northern slope, the carpet of fallen leaves has been disturbed here and there by hungry squirrels in search of hidden prizes. In other places, long swathes of leaves lie disturbed in wandering lines, revealing the dark humus beneath, perhaps the actions of foraging badgers.

Further up the sloping path a little way ahead, shafts of orange winter sun traverse the ground, and on the Knott, the summit is painted gold by the same winter sun hovering just above the canopies in the west. What limited warmth it provides, although welcome, is stripped away by a strong, northerly breeze bringing down final remnant leaves. Long, silken threads flash silver in the air, agitated by the breeze.

I leave the top and enter the shade and chill of the southern slope. Urgent barking sounds out, jarring and intrusive, and I stop to listen. Before too long, two roe deer emerge hurriedly from cover and head up and out of sight over the Knott. They are followed a short while later by a determined grey, short-coated dog, nose to ground and on the hunt. To the south, hidden by the trees, its owner calls out and I meet him a little while later by the Great Beech and advise him of his dog's antics. He continues calling as I head west. I think the deer are safe.

On my way through the rhododendron glade, a flock of long-tailed tits crosses my path in the air in front of me, chattering as they go. Perhaps the same flock that provided much-needed inspiration a couple of entries back. About where our very young beech fades steadily to yellow, I move off path, down the slope heading north, along a well-trodden and narrow game trail. I pass by horizontal branches and whole trunks decorated in thick blankets of lush green moss. A little further on, and remaining off path, I enter a graveyard of decaying fallen giants. Massive trunks lay spent and ruined in the tangle of bracken and bramble. Out of the corner of my eye, I spy what I initially take to be a large grey fungus, but as I draw closer, it is far from that. On a fallen mossy branch, an upright squirrel enjoys a late afternoon lunch of cream-coloured chestnut, clasped between agile forepaws. His raised, bushy tail follows the curve of his bent back and protrudes comically, flag-like, above his grey head. Black eyes regard me cautiously, but my approach does not cause alarm. To my surprise, I close within a matter of feet of this squirrel, seemingly more interested in eating than fleeing. I stop and together we watch each other for a while, before I turn my back and move slowly away, making my way around and over fallen trunk and branch.

I continue through the tangle of branches before the going becomes a little easier and find myself with a clear stream to my left, flowing between steep-sided, leaf-strewn banks. I follow its course and a short while later arrive at the familiar confluence.

The dog remains on the hunt; the owner's calls echo distantly through the wood as I leave.

SIXTY

MOTHER OF THE WOOD

Sunday, 8 December 2019 – 14.00

The close-cropped parkland grass is buffeted and rippled in waves by the wind racing. Gold and brown leaves are carried, scudding hurriedly over the grass to come to rest in drifts and windrows. As I make my way up the long, steady sweep of hillside, the wild wind roars in the naked branches of the sentinel oaks and beeches away ahead. The sky above the landscaped horizon is a patchwork of cold blue and ragged shower cloud. A watery sun in the west pokes apologetically between the clouds over my left shoulder, hanging low above the spreading cedar.

I have the wide wooded world to myself.

I pass the head of the Down and drop down the intimate narrow path to the confines of the wood and find relief from the wind. I pass a straggling herb Robert still in stubborn flower –

a bright flash of pink, and the stump puff balls spotted entries back now look worse for wear, but they have been productive, shooting forth the next generation.

I turn right, following the toe of the deer bank heading east. The strong, blustery winds have stripped the very last of the stubborn leaves from the canopies and the treetops are now fully winter bare. The wood is altogether more open. Only the young, low beech trees are reluctant to shake off their golden coat; their dried, curled leaves rattle and rasp in the winter wind, whispering their secret language.

I spot the mature domed holly high up the deer bank, dark and brooding against the backdrop of the towering veteran beech behind. The beech's network of skeletal branches reaches out from its forked trunk to touch the winter blue. My curiosity is piqued, and I strike off path in the direction of the holly and beech, up the steadily rising slope. Over the flattened bracken. I have not gone far up the slope before I spot brown subtle movement a little way off to my right. Amongst the bracken, an antlered head rises. It is a roe buck, the first I can recall seeing up the wood. He is alone and watchful. I stand stock still and raise the camera slowly, but he is a long way off and I only manage one blurry shot before he bounds urgently away.

The beech sits atop the very edge of the bank, teetering on the precipice. I scramble up the fanned out network of gnarly roots that creep, serpent-like, over the ground, seeking shallow purchase. Upon closer inspection, this forked veteran could be a candidate for the mantle of the new Great Beech. A little of the Mother of the Wood now.

The beech trees present in significant numbers in our wood are the species known as common beech, also known as European beech (*Fagus sylvatica*). The bark of the beech is typically smooth and light grey in colour. The leaves are ovate in shape and between five and seven centimetres in length. In the spring, the leaves emerge soft and supple in vibrant lime green. At this stage in the life of the leaf, they are soft enough to eat, and some say they have a hint of lemon. They can be plucked from the tree sparingly and consumed on the go or gathered for use in a wild salad. Later on, the leaves turn dark green and have a robust, waxy texture. In the autumn, as we have recently observed, the leaves put on a dazzling display of gold.

The fruit of the beech is known as the mast. The triangular-shaped red-brown nuts develop in spikey hardwood nut cases – the *mast* – which, in the autumn, litter the woodland floor in their tens of thousands below the canopies. I noticed on my way up through the parkland today that on the veteran beech trees, whilst the network of branches and twigs are bare, much of the mast remains. The years where the beech produces the mast is, or rather was, known as 'mast years'. Wohlleben comments that every five years, a beech tree produces a harvest of thirty thousand beech nuts, and over its life, this equates to 1.8 million beech nuts, one of which will grow into the next generation. Wohlleben also observes that the raucous jay assists with the next generation of beech trees through gathering the nuts and burying them throughout the wood.

From my own observations, the wood has a healthy stock of juvenile beech (but not a profusion, tending to add weight to Wohlleben's thoughts) waiting, pensive but patient. Only a short distance along the top of the deer bank from the veteran that I am currently stood under, there is a tiny beech sapling, maybe two years old, growing around thirty centimetres high. Its six golden leaves are all arranged facing due south, and the space above the sapling is conveniently clear. And alongside its winter leaves, pointy, red-coloured buds already hold next spring's foliage. If fate allows, in a couple of hundred years from now, this sapling will stand tall and proud.

Beech can grow up to forty metres in height at full maturity, and they have a rounded crown, but I have observed that some of the sentinel beeches in the parkland have a tall, slender shape. Beech is a native of southern England, with its natural range extending up to a line drawn between the Wash and the river Severn. Consequently, further north than this, the beech is considered to be non-native. It is said that the beech is the Mother of the Wood, or the Beech Queen to the Oak King. In folklore, the spreading beech tree would provide safe shelter and protection to the weary traveller. You will recall that only recently, a juvenile beech provided sufficient shelter for me for a time from a short rain shower.

I drop down the slope, carefully back over the beech roots, and continue on.

I spot an oddity at the base of the slope, a short distance from the beech; it is hard to describe, but it is almost a wall of roots, around a metre high and one and a half metres long – the roots belong to a semi-mature sycamore which has succumbed to the wind and now lies horizontal across the woodland floor. But the tangled, intertwining wall of roots are healthy and still partly embedded in the rich humus. And from the horizontal trunk, what would have otherwise been a branch is now a juvenile trunk in its own right, springing up, mast-straight.

I head back up the bank and traverse the slope, just below its summit. Our lone larch, now winter bare, is ahead, and with the bracken died down, I can investigate a little more without struggle. The growth of the larch has been stunted by an intertwined beech tree which has caused the larch to bend double so that its one-sided canopy weeps down the slope. And below this weeping canopy is a grotto – its roof is the dense network of larch branches which, even though bare, create a nearly unbroken ceiling. Below this, the sloped floor is a solid carpet of accumulated beech leaves. A fine room indeed.

I rejoin the deer bank summit and continue heading east. I have two, what must be, final fungi to describe for you. They are very worthy of mention. The first, growing atop a decaying log, is a tight cluster of really what look like purple pebbles, with a combined length of around ten centimetres and width of between five and seven centimetres. According to the Amanita photo guide (my own guide is silent), this is the purple jelly disc fungus (*Ascocoryne sarcoides*), and this particular specimen is in its early form; the purple pebbles will flatten out soon to form shallow, cup-shaped discs, hence the name.

A little further on, similarly growing on top of a decaying log, is a bright yellow fungus, which looks a little like a crumpled up piece of yellow cellophane. The fruiting body has had the strength to lift up the bark of the log. This is the yellow brain fungus (*Tremella mesenterica*). According to my guide, the yellow brain fungus grows on fallen deciduous branches and is gelatinous in appearance in damp conditions but becomes hard and shrivelled in dry conditions and consequently is harder to spot.

I continue on.

On the Knott, the rope swings sway in the wind, forlorn and unused.

Commentators have suggested that the origin of the word 'book' may be derived from the name 'beech'. In Germany for example, the words for 'book' and 'beech' are very similar. It is thought that the apparent association stems from the use of beech tablets for writing before the advent of other writing materials. The association may even be derived from the practice of carving words, possibly even runes and ogham, into the thin bark of the beech. Certainly, the two beeches on the summit of the Knott are tattooed with a hectic array of initials and symbols incised in the soft bark by visitors over the years. Expressions of love figure prominently with at least three drawn hearts containing the initials of smitten couples.

And alongside these symbols of undying love are simply the initials of the scribe, my favourite being 'JM', dated 1924, representing the earliest discernible inscription. The style of the lettering appears contemporary with that period and the initials have been carved with care. The number '4' is more traced with a fingertip than seen.

In researching the folklore of the beech, I have stumbled across the story of a particular beech that was clearly as important to many people as the Great Beech was to me and my family. Sitting atop Castle Hill, part of the Wittenham Clumps in the county of Oxfordshire, there stood until 2012, The Poem Tree – a beech tree into which Joseph Tubb carved a poem in the 1840s.

> *As up the hill with lab'ring steps we tread*
> *Where the twin Clumps their sheltering branches spread*
> *The summit gain'd at ease reclining lay*
> *And all around the widespread scene survey*
> *Point out each object and instructive tell*
> *The various changes that the land befell*
> *Where the low bank the country wide surrounds*
> *That ancient earthwork form'd old Mercia's bounds*
> *In misty distance see the barrow heave*
> *There lies forgotten lonely Cwichelm's grave.*
> *Around this hill the ruthless Danes intrenched*
> *And these fair plains with gory slaughter drench'd*
> *While at our feet where stands that stately tower*

In days gone by up rose the Roman power
And yonder, there where Thames smooth waters glide
In later days appeared monastic pride.
Within that field where lies the grazing herd
Huge walls were found, some coffins disinter'd
Such is the course of time, the wreck which fate
And awful doom award the earthly great.

All that on a lofty beech.

I drop down the western side of the Knott and through the patch of juvenile and mature hollies, many still in red berry. I am minded to name this pocket the 'hollywood'. Beyond the hollies, and unnoticed by me previously, is a steep-sided gulley, through which flows a narrow, clear stream. Even now, after all this time, there are still new discoveries to be made. I cross to its opposite bank and in doing so, very nearly lose my welly in the soft stream bed. I decide to track its course upstream out of curiosity in an attempt to find its source. After other careful crossings and scrambles though scrub and over fallen trees, eventually – after a hundred or so yards – I arrive at a point where the stream's crystal clear waters emerge magically from the woodland floor. This is the only spring that I am aware of within the wood.

I continue on through unfamiliar surroundings off path but heading steadily west, across gullies, around deadfalls and avoiding the worst of the bramble. I flush out muntjac and cause complaining blackbirds to take short, streaking flights. My way takes me north of the spreading patch of rhododendrons, and I spy them through the trunks, a dark green band distinct against the brown backdrop. A familiar feature seen from a new perspective. Hereabouts, the wood guards well a secret that I will not share.

Eventually, I leave the shelter of the wood and offer myself to the unabated roar of the wind. The nearly full moon, silver against the later afternoon blue, keeps me company as I make my way back down through the sentinel beeches.

SIXTY-ONE

FATHER OF THE WOOD

Sunday, 15 December 2019 – 13.00

The village church bells musically strike one o'clock as Jim Bob and I make our way down the valley. We are walking into the low winter sun; silver pinpricks of light dance in the air ahead. The bare branches and twigs in the hedgerow are decorated with glossy red rosehips and the green-brown catkins of the hazel. Yellow crab apples, bauble-like, adorn bare branches.

We enter the wood at the north-western corner, through the kissing gate, and make our way steadily eastwards. I show Jim the yellow brain fungus spotted last week – still vibrant yellow – but we somehow manage to miss the purple jelly disc.

We eventually find ourselves on the Knott. If the Mother of the Wood is the beech, then the oak is most certainly the Father of the Wood. And the oak atop the Knott, whilst it may not be the oldest, has a high and central setting which must surely set it apart from all of its subjects. The oak is as much a part of the British consciousness as Big Ben or Stonehenge. The wood, from its robust boughs and strong trunks, has built the ships that have defended our island home; its timbers line the walls of our seats of power, and its enduring strength is the framework that provides us shelter. Its symbols even adorn the change in our pockets. It is appropriate then that as we draw near the end (we are, after all, very close), I tell you something of the much-revered oak now.

We already know, and as has already been observed by Mr Simms back at the midpoint of the last century, that our wood is known for its dominant pedunculate oak or English oak (*Quercus robur*) as it is better known. The English oak grows to a height of around thirty-six metres and has a spreading, rambling crown of heavy branches. The bark of the oak is grey and becomes deeply fissured with time, and its symbolic leaves are deeply lobed and grow from short stalks – no more than five millimetres in length. The fruit of the oak is the acorn which grows on long stalks and comprises the scaly, perfect cup and cylindrical, rounded, smooth nut, vibrant green in colour. The acorns grow in singles, pairs or clusters of three. The pedunculate oak is native to Britain and distributed widely throughout our Isles.

Kings have taken refuge in their boughs, and monarchs have danced and picnicked below their rambling canopies. Outlaws have camped under its protection, and courts have sat in judgement within its shade. The long-living oak is so much a part of us that over time, we have named individual memorable trees throughout this land that either stand the test of time or have been lost but are still fondly remembered. Here are just a few of their number.

The Cowthorpe Oak

I start with the Cowthorpe Oak because, by all accounts, it holds the crown for having had the greatest girth of any English Oak in the British Isles, measured at 14.32 metres at 1.8 metres off the ground in the year 1804. Legend has it that seventy people were able to squeeze into its ancient, hollowed out, dark interior, although part of that number was made up of children perched on grown-ups' shoulders. The tree stood for maybe around one thousand years until it was felled in 1950.

The Cowthorpe Oak was immortalised by William Shakespeare in *As You Like It* with the following words:

> *An oak whose boughs were mossed with age, and high top bald with dry antiquity.*

The Bowthorpe Oak

The next memorable oak in my short list is the Bowthorpe Oak located at Bowthorpe Park Farm, Manthorpe, Lincolnshire. Along with the Fredville Oak in the county of Kent, the Bowthorpe Oak holds the record for being the largest girthed oak still standing in the British Isles at 12.3 metres and is said to be at least one thousand years old.

The Queen's Oak

Until 1997, the Queen's Oak stood close to the village of Potterspury, in Northamptonshire, not too far from our wood. Folklore has it that King Edward IV met his future Queen, Elizabeth Woodville, the mother of the 'Princes in the Tower', within the spread of the Queen's Oak on 13 April 1464.

In the year 1879, the girth of the Queen's Oak was measured at 6.83 metres.

Herne's Oak

Windsor Great Park, originally part of the great Windsor Forest, lays claim to several hundred ancient oak trees, including named oaks, the most famous of which is arguably Herne's Oak which stood until 1796 and was immortalised by William Shakespeare in *The Merry Wives of Windsor* with the following words:

> *There is an old tale goes that Herne the Hunter,*
> *Sometime a keeper here in Windsor Forest,*
> *Doth all the winter time, at still midnight,*
> *Walk round about an oak, with great ragg'd horns;*
> *And there he blasts the tree and takes the cattle*
> *And makes milchekine yield blood, and shakes the chain*
> *In a most hideous and dreadful manner:*
> *You have heard of such a spirit, and well you know*
> *The superstitious idle-headed eld*
> *Received and did deliver to our age,*
> *This tale of Herne the Hunter for a truth.*

We leave the Oak King behind and make our way down the wild western slope off path, through the hollywood and onto the recently discovered stream, where I show Jim its source. As we stop to gaze into its clear waters bubbling up from buried ironstone, a jay utters its harsh call from the treetops high above us. Now the canopies are bare, I am able to get a good look at this most colourful and illusive member of the crow family; my first observation is of the dull pink plumage of its chest. The jay is high up, but I can just make out (with the aid of my monocular) the black and white speckles of its head, its robust, short beak and the blue flash on its wing edge. The jay continues to call and gestures in warning with its dark tail feathers.

We continue heading west off path. In amongst a tangle of bramble and bracken, Jim Bob spots the briefest glimpse of a small grey mouse. I am quite jealous.

There are many poems about the Father of the Wood, but the following is my favourite:

Live thy Life,
Young and old,
Like yon oak,
Bright in spring
Living gold;

Summer-rich
Then; and then
Autumn-changed
Soberer-hued
Gold again.

All his leaves
Fall'n at length,
Look, he stands,
Trunk and bough
Naked strength

The Oak
Alfred Lord Tennyson

SIXTY-TWO

OF MIDWINTER

Sunday, 22 December 2019 – 14.30

It is a little over an hour from sunset on the shortest day of the year. It is the winter solstice, and the dark is rising.

I am reacquainted with Teddy at the beginning of today's visit, only this time, he is more interested in deciphering canine messages from around the base of a tall oak and consequently much less interested in me. His mum and I exchange season's greetings and comment on Teddy's questionable character.

I continue on over the pasture, unnoticed and unmolested. In the ridge and furrow, industrious moles have left a miniature landscape of dotted orange spoil heaps in the green grass. From the upper pasture, The Oak King and the beech crowning Knobbly Knott stand out proud on the far winter horizon; their canopies silhouetted black against a flat, grey sky.

Within the wood, the vista is muted winter tones and monochrome. The closing of the year and the short days have leeched the very last of the colour. The muddy path winds its course in front of me, and I follow, slipping and sliding, churning the already churned surface. I turn east onto the partially metalled, only slightly less muddy, path, despite the ancient, time-worn stones laid haphazard along its surface. The rain-swollen stream babbles along its course to my right for a time.

I follow the now well-trodden diversion around the recently fallen oak, its flanks stained dark by the weather, and then continue on, making my way slowly eastwards, exchanging a 'hello' with another lone walker, before arriving at the main track; with the winter die back, the track is broad, and away off to my left, the arch is revealed; shallow, water-filled ruts taper to the clear space below its time-eroded stonework.

I cross the track and head off path, treading purposefully through the bramble and up the leaf-strewn ground beneath towering pines. Squirrels chatter and squabble in the high branches. There is just the odd decaying fungus amongst the leaf litter – exposed gills curl upwards and stalks are canted over. I catch a glimpse of salmon pink on the side of a decaying wild cherry stump; it is a splash of colour against the background of dark, mouldering bark and green, speckled lichen. It is a small mass of really what looks like fish eggs on pale short stalks. I think this is raspberry slime mould (*Tubifera ferruginosa*). Raspberry slime mould grows in tightly packed clusters, often having the appearance of a raspberry, hence the name. The hunt is finally over then.

I continue on, steadily rising past myriad ancient warrens and one well-used warren, past the rediscovered hollow, now water-filled, and through the pines that gradually give way to the high beeches. Through the trunks in the west, the orange winter sun sits level with the near horizon. A bright orange disk radiating light through the hundreds of trunks. I join a path and drop steadily down the slope; the golden disk, flickering, keeps pace with my every stride. It lights up the western flanks of beech all around me and washes gold over the woodland floor, pushing back the searching dark.

We are only a short time before sunset. I pause at the five-bar gate to watch the sun's slow, bright descent into winter embers; for a brief moment, he rests, caught in the forked trunk of the nearest sentinel oak, bright fire between black trunk, branch and twig.

I carry on along old, familiar ways in the last light of midwinter. By way of farewell, as I draw near the once Great Beech, the buzzard, the jackdaw, crow and blackbird herald the end of the shortest day. And somewhere, far off in the wild wood, they are joined by Bran.

So the shortest day came, and the year died,
And everyone down the centuries of the snow-white world
Came people singing, dancing,
To drive the dark away.
They lighted candles in the winter trees;
They hung their homes with evergreen;
They burned beseeching fires all night long
To keep the year alive.
And when the new year's sunshine blazed awake
They shouted, revelling.
Through all the frosty ages you can hear them
Echoing, behind us – listen!
All the long echoes sing the same delight,

This shortest day,
As promise wakens in the sleeping land:
They carol, feast, give thanks,
And dearly love their friends, and hope for peace.
And so do we, here, now,
This year, and every year.
Welcome, Yule!

The Shortest Day
Susan Cooper

SIXTY-THREE
OF HOLLY AND YULE

Christmas Eve 2019 – 15.10

The evergreen tree and its ancient magic, welcome in our home for the darkest days at the end of the year, stands decorated for all to see. This day is full of promise of the festival ahead, but our family traditions are not yet quite complete.

We head through the arch, perhaps for the last time on this journey – we shall see. As we enter the confines of the Winter Wood and welcome her familiar embrace, the Christingle bells in the squat square tower of the distant church sound out clear and in perfect accompaniment. I am joined today by Em on this, our yearly Christmas Eve vigil, to gather the final tokens for our festive season. We make our way, without hurry, along the main track, trying our best to avoid the worst of the deep, clinging mud, before conceding defeat and instead heading below empty canopies off the path and over the leaf litter. After a time, and deep in conversation, we meet the clear path that will carry us to the heart of the wood.

Just short of the summit, a long-fallen beech is laid out over the woodland floor. This is our first destination today, as it has been for a long time on each Christmas Eve. This is our true 'Christmas tree'. At the end of its long, dark, barkless trunk, the beech's impotent ancient roots, wrenched forth from the ground, reach high over our heads. I give due thanks and carefully remove a length of cold, damp root; below the soft exterior, the heartwood is strong, and it will burn slowly tonight in our hearth, lit from the scorched remnant of last year's log, providing welcome warmth and light, while the family busies around making final preparations.

On the Knott, Em, as she has always done, whatever age, swings to and fro below the empty sky with broad smile to match my own. Down its western slope, Em catches the briefest glimpse of a wood rabbit, startled and fleeting. We make our way in that direction, down through the hollywood, where we pause to reverently gather holly sprigs – the final ritual. Their spikey, dark green leaves will rest on the mantle pieces and above the threshold. Along with the wreath and the Christmas tree, with its delicate glass baubles, these evergreen symbols, older than time, will keep the dark at bay over the long, dark nights ahead.

With the backdrop of the bells drifting perfectly through the acres of wood, and with the yule log and holly in hand, we reluctantly leave her embrace to join the final preparations at home.

SIXTY-FOUR

OF JOURNEY'S END

New Year's Eve – 07.25

It is the last day of 2019, the last day of the decade and the last entry in this journal of the wood. I arrive at the greens under a blue-black early morning sky, a little over half an hour from the sunrise. The windows of the cottages lining the greens remain mainly dark this New Year's Eve morning. There is just the odd warm glow from behind pulled drapes. Holly wreaths adorn wood-panelled front doors, holding the dark at bay. The birds are up though, and there is a dawn chorus in the low light, sung in earnest by robin and blackbird.

I pass the Victorian church, its robust red brick facades coloured orange from the light cast by a solitary street light. Out in the ridge and furrow, as I emerge through the ornate metal kissing gate, the western horizon, glimpsed through the distant black silhouettes of the trees lining the lane, glows dawn orange.

Within the wood, the hour belongs to the birds of all kinds heralding the start of the last day. I head west, over the streams and along the western and then southern edge. Whilst I know with certainty that I will be back here in this space, in my wood again, probably as soon as Sunday, I do nevertheless have the sense of saying 'thanks' and 'farewell', a strong desire to revisit, for one final time, those 'woodmarks' that have become familiar over the preceding year.

My first stop is the rhododendron glade, all browns and blacks now, compared to the white, frigid world of a couple of weeks ago and the vibrant green space that it was only really a few weeks before that. Now, the bright pink flowers are a distant memory, the bracken lays flattened and ruinous and the trees are bare. Even the marble galls on the juvenile oak have gone (I can only think that they have been taken as a souvenir). And this pocket of sky around and above me, previously busy with erratic butterflies and hawking dragonflies, watched over by the soaring buzzards, is an empty and restful space.

The night is giving way by degrees to the day and an ever-lightening sky.

I want to join the most southerly of paths at the toe of the deer bank, away to my right and so head due south on the rising ground, over the dead bracken which crinkles and crackles audibly under each footfall. I join the path only a short distance from the shrine, our next marker, and this time I happen to have, almost by intention, a pre-decimalisation penny in my trouser pocket. I place the time-worn coin reverently amongst the collection of other copper and silver coins spread out in haphazard fashion over the small, cluttered altartop. And, as I stand on the brink of a new decade, I wish for those most basic of human desires for family and friends. Perhaps, after all, that is what this space is simply about.

I continue on, along the rich, dark, sticky path. About where the formal path leads out into the parkland, I stop one final time to listen to the susurrations of the young, leaf-clad beech, and I hear its winter lament. All while a solitary song thrush away to my right sings in rich silvers and golds. I notice a game trail leading up through the bracken to the very top of the deer bank a little way ahead, and I follow its course over brown stems worn in flat, orderly, parallel lines over the surface of the narrow trail by myriad paws.

From the long ridge on the wood edge, the fully light landscape to the south reveals itself to be overcast and misty winter grey. Between the bank edge and the fenced parkland, there is a deep, bramble-free dry ditch, which I drop down into. Its surface, too, is also well trodden by beasts. I follow its narrow, sunken route for a time, past gnarly oak and beech, their limbs twisted and directionless, with old scars stained dark and exposed trunks leaning precariously.

On the leaf-filled path, a little way ahead, lifeless, circular sockets gaze up at me from bleached white bone long picked bare. And a little further on, an equally bare jointed backbone lies at a right angle across the base of the ditch; articulated ribs, bright white, point skywards. Fore and hindlegs must be abroad somewhere, long lost. Food for the birds and the beasts.

I continue on, along the intimate confines of the sunken path, the sweep of the wood below to my left and the open expanse of the parkland and its sentinels to my right, out of sight. Eventually, the cutting levels out. I traverse carefully over the serpentine spread of beech roots cascading down over the bank edge and past the still vibrant yellow brain fungus. The game trail along the very top of the ridge leads me on, eastwards, to the next marker: our familiar Great Beech. Laid carefully against the side of the great, ragged stump, cerise pink carnations on long, green stems rest in remembrance. And deep within the hollow stump, a single red rose is symbolic of enduring love. I wonder what sad story they tell.

The Knott is calling, and I must pay homage to the Oak King. One final time. From the top, I watch as a mixed flock of tits moves to and fro with purpose, foraging in the tangles of bracken and bramble. Around the sycamores and chestnuts, and on the edge of the hollywood, squirrels, maybe as many as five or six, chase in twos and threes over the woodland floor and scamper up and down grey trunks.

I leave the Knott and head down its eastern slope, past our 'Christmas tree', its remnant scorched root now carefully saved at home to light next year's yule log. On a whim and knowing that there is one place that we must visit on this our farewell journey, I take a side path leading due south. I find that the topography and landform in the extent of the wood can sometimes be hard to discern. It must be because visibility is sometimes limited by the dense mass of trunks and underlying scrub, but here, as I head down the side path, the trees thin and visibility over distance increases – it is not quite a glade but rather an area that is more open, and we are able to observe that it is a sweep of shallow valley dotted with trees. As I make my way, and almost appropriately, I cause a small herd of roe deer emerging out of the scrub to take flight, as they always do; I watch them bound away, white rumps mesmerising before they are lost in amongst the firs on the opposite side of the valley. They are the wild. I follow in their general direction, but I shall not see them again.

I enter the gloom of the firs on the far side of the valley, where light is limited below their dense, evergreen drooping boughs. I move out of the firs and into the naked beeches and then past the cypress. I stop awhile and listen one last time to the whisper of the breeze through their dense, evergreen canopies. And away in the distance, beyond the wood edge and out in the parkland, there is the definite croak of our friend Bran but barely heard over the cacophony of the excitable jackdaws.

I continue on, steadily rising along the twisting path. The ruin is glimpsed for a final time between the trunks a long way off to our right. After a short while, I arrive at our penultimate marker and rest for a time, leaning on the smooth wood of the top rail. I will see this view again, but for you reader, this is the final time. I watch as clatterings of jackdaws, many in number, gather together, swooping in black masses between the sentinel oak and beech. I have this space entirely to myself and smile fondly at recalled memories of aerobatic bats and dragonflies (that never came) and the whoosh of Bran on black wings, the silver haloed ewe, the briefest glimpse of a hare and the deer in the dark. It is a magical spot, and I will never tire of it.

I leave the five-bar gate behind and head up into the high beeches and then along the long path running parallel to the northern edge, which eventually leads us to our final destination: the familiar ancient arch. Our portal out away from the wild and back to our everyday lives. Just as I am about to leave, I spy a honeysuckle entwined clockwise around a young sycamore; delicate green leaves – new life, freshly emerged – sprout forth from its sinuous twisting stems. We have come full circle.

It is clear to me now, at the end, that before our year-long journey, I had largely been a passer-by, inattentive and mostly blind in my wanderings, but I have now had the privilege of observing the wood for all that it is, its secrets and its stories revealed.

The End
4 January 2020

END NOTES

It has been suggested to me by some, but not all, that *Of the Wood* would benefit from photographs to accompany the text. *Of the Wood* was never meant to be a field guide as such. I always wanted it to be experience and observation by amateur eyes translated into the written word. There are countless field guides out there and some are mentioned in the bibliography. Dip into those if you feel the need. Otherwise, you are welcome to visit my Instagram page which is almost entirely made up of photographs of the flora, fauna, fungi and lichens of the wood: #_of_the_wood_

And finally, I cannot go without saying thank you to the following. My friends Glen (Gup), Gary (Gazza) and Mike for humouring me and patiently reading drafts and for providing helpful feedback. Thanks also to Mr Irving, my friendly ecologist colleague who assisted with identification and general fact-checking. And thank you to Susan Cooper for allowing me to give a nod to certain characters and quotes from *The Dark Is Rising Sequence* (my most favourite adventure and which set me on a life-long passion for the magic world of story) and for inclusion of Susan's poem *The Shortest Day*.

Badby Wood is privately owned, and it is only the willingness and grace of its owner that allows the public access, myself included. Please do not take it for granted and respect the clearly stated 'Private Property' signs.

Roy Hammond
May 2021

BIBLIOGRAPHY AND
FURTHER READING

Arlot, Fitter and Fitter, *The Complete Guide to British Wildlife*, Collins (1981).

Blamey, Fitter, *Collins Gem Guide – Wild Flowers*, Harper Collins Publishers (1980).

Blanchan, *Wild Flowers Worth Knowing* (1917).

Campbell, *The Gaelic Otherworld*,

Birlinn, General, Clarke, *Mushrooms and Fungi*, Usborne Publishing Ltd (1980).

Chinery, *Wildlife of Britain and Europe*, Kingfisher Publications Plc (1987).

Dobson, *Lichens – An Illustrated Guide to the British and Irish Species*, The Richmond Publishing Company Limited (2011).

Fitzsimons, Forey, *Edible Plants*, Brockhampton Press (2000).

Fletcher, *Wildflowers*, Dorling Kindersley (2004).

Graves, *The White Goddess*, Faber & Faber Ltd (1961).

Hight, *Britain's Tree Story*, National Trust (2011).

Howard, *Traditional Folk Remedies*, Century Paperbacks (1987).

Mabey, *Collins Gem – Food for Free*, Harper Collins Publishers (2004).

Mabey, *Flora Britannica*, Chatto & Windus (1996).

Mears, Hillman, *Wild Food*, Hodder & Stoughton Ltd (2007).

Mears, *Bushcraft*, Hodder & Stoughton Ltd (2002).

Roud, *The Penguin guide to the Superstitions of Britain and Ireland*, Penguin (2003).

Roud, *A Pocket Guide to Superstitions of the British Isles*, Penguin Books (2004).

Simms, *Woodland Birds*, Collins (1971).

Sterry, *Collins Complete British Trees*, Harper Collins Publishers (2007).

Svrcek, *A Field Guide in Colour to Mushrooms*, Silverdale Books (2000).

Williams, *Oak-galls in Britain – Volume 1* (2010).

Wohlleben, *The Hidden Life of Trees*, William Collins (2017).

Online Resources

www.amanita-photolibrary.co.uk – fungi identification.

www.britishbugs.org.uk – insect identification.

www.wdvta.org.uk – for aging trees.

www.orthoptera.org.uk – for grasshopper and related insect identification.

www.british-dragonflies.org.uk – for damselfly and dragonfly identification.

www.plant-lore.com – for the folklore and uses of plants.

www.wikipedia.org – for just about everything wood and wildlife related (amongst other things).

www.ancienttreeforum.org.uk – for the celebration, protection and enjoyment of our old trees.